AF270800

Richard Scott Griffin, Mount Holly, NC
North Carolina Teacher of the Year, 1996
Teaches grades 4–6—all subject areas
Served as Teacher Advisor to State
Board of Education

Rob O'Leary, Sidney, OH
School principal
Former fourth-grade teacher
Fellowship Award recipient from
Wright State University

Denise Johnson, New York, NY
Teacher Center Specialist in
Manhattan
Previously taught grades 4–8
Instructor at Brooklyn College

Jenlane Gee Matt, Modesto, CA
California Teacher of the Year, 1988
National Teacher of the Year
finalist, 1989
Third-grade teacher

Norma Jackson, Keller, TX
Texas Teacher of the Year, 1999
On special assignment as District Writing
Specialist for grades K–5
Second-grade teacher
Summer Activity Writing Specialist

Linda Ullah, Santa Clara, CA
Harold H. Hailer Award in
Instructional Technology
Former Special Education, Gifted and
Talented Education, Title 1 teacher
Technology and learning specialist
Teacher in Residence, Foothill College
Krause Center for Innovation

Vered Raz, New York, NY
Fine arts educator
Arts Education Research,
University Settlement
Former elementary school teacher

Carol Caverley, Acton, ON
Elementary School Principal
Course Instructor of Additional Qualifications
for Teachers: Literacy and Primary Education
Former Curriculum Program Consultant,
Junior Kindergarten to Grade 3

Please contact us at:
Attn: Summer Vacation, Entertainment Publications,
1414 E. Maple Road, Troy, Michigan 48083 or
e-mail us at: **summervacation@entertainment.com.**

Eveonne T. Lockhart, Cupertino, CA
Excellence in Education
Former 2nd and 3rd grade teacher
Middle School teacher

Grade 6 Skills

The sixth grade will be an exciting and potentially frustrating year as your child enters adolescence. His or her growing autonomy will be illustrated by a growing self-assertion and curiosity. Sixth-grade teachers work to increase students' proficiency in basic skills. Organization will be critical as your child begins to have a different teacher for each subject. By the end of the sixth grade, your child may be able to:

- use similes, metaphors, and personification to enhance writing.
- identify and incorporate first-person and third-person point of view in literature and writing.
- use base words, word endings and beginnings, and context clues to decode.
- demonstrate the use of the writing process.
- use research skills to write detailed reports.
- interpret graphs.
- plot coordinates and ordered pairs on a graph.
- find the radius, diameter, and circumference of circles.
- apply abstract reasoning to solve simple algebraic equations.
- work with ratios, proportions, and percents.

How You Can Help

You can help prepare your child for sixth grade by making this Summer Vacation® book a regular part of your daily routine. Assist your child in the construction of the airplane models and with the additional research and writing activities. Share in the reading of the stories found in this book as a vehicle for discussion and to model reading as an enjoyable experience in your life. The Summer Vacation book is designed to help your child retain the skills that he or she developed in fifth grade and to prepare him or her for the challenges of sixth grade.

Hudson's Children

CHAPTER ONE

Cold air poured from the air-conditioning, and Trekk was happy to lie there and let the cool wave wash over him. The day, like the summer, stretched out in front of him with no schedules, no demands, and no need even to see what day it was. "This is great," Trekk thought.

Most summers, it was go, go, go. For as long as Trekk could remember, he and his cousin Terra had spent summers together, finding one adventure after the next. Terra's mother was an archaeologist from New Mexico, and they had been to several of her digs in the Southwest. Other summers they'd been with Trekk's dad, a writer, as he took working vacations to do research on articles he wrote for a New York newspaper.

This year, though, everybody was staying home. Terra's mom was finishing a report on her work, and Trekk's dad had nothing special to do. Trekk felt bad about not missing Terra more, but he was also looking forward to just hanging with his friends. He'd been practicing three-sixties on his skateboard, and he knew that when he landed in sixth grade this fall, he would be landing the jump as well.

"Trekk, wake up. I have news." Trekk roused himself. Was it lunchtime? "I have news," Dad repeated. "We'll see Terra after all."

"Huh? We will?" Trekk responded groggily. "Uh…why?"

"Her mom got a chance to go to Peru. She's going to excavate ruins in the mountains. So Terra's going to be with us."

"Oh. Cool. Okay," Trekk said, but he wondered how the energetic Terra would fit in with his friends and his plans for goofing off. "When does she get here?"

"She doesn't," Dad said. "That's part two of the news. We'll pick her up. I've been assigned to research and report on Henry Hudson."

"Who's Henry Hudson?" Trekk asked. "And what are you supposed to write about him?"

"Hudson, like the river," Dad said. "And I haven't any idea what to write about yet. I'm sure I'll know what direction to take once our research is underway."

Trekk groaned. "Who wants to study a dirty old river?" he asked.

"Not the river," Dad grinned, "the Bay. We'll meet Terra in Michigan, and then head north."

"North? What's north of Michigan? Canada?" Trekk was having trouble taking it all in at once.

"Exactly," Dad said. "Western Ontario to be precise. What information do you know," he dragged out poetically, "about the province of Ontario?"

"I'm not sure I know enough about Ontario to be much help," Trekk chimed back. "Can I bring my skateboard?" Dad smiled, more or less.

"Better start packing," he said.

Trekk decided to make the best of it. "Maybe we can come up with an idea for you," he said.

"I'd love it," Dad said. "But even if you don't, I promise you adventure."

Invest In Your Child's Future

Dear Parents,

Did you know that your children can lose up to 25 percent of their reading and math skills during summer vacation? Or that children whose schools incorporate project-based learning perform 26 percent better on standardized tests?

While children enjoy the summer break, they experience summer learning loss if they don't practice their skills. That is why we created Summer Vacation®—a fun, entertaining educational program to prevent summer learning loss.

The Summer Vacation Grade 6 Activity Book is packed with new, fun activities that will help your children succeed in school:

- New, teacher-approved activities that meet national curriculum standards
- All-new language and math exercises to prepare your child for the challenges of grade 6
- Fun word problems using addition, subtraction, multiplication and division
- Brain teasers and logic problems
- Motivating, skill-building activities that address a variety of learning styles to make learning fun and exciting
- All-new project section—"Discover Flight"—that your child can do all summer long
- Removable "history of flight" charts

*__Summer Vacation__ has the **highest** satisfaction **rating** (94% of consumers satisfied) **compared** to all other educational products tested including **LeapPad**®, **JumpStart**® Software, and **Scholastic**® Activity Kits. Source: EPI Consumer Behavior Study, Market Tools, Inc. 2004

Although we've organized the book around daily lessons, your children can complete most of the exercises independently and work at the pace that's most comfortable for them.

Take a look at Grade 6's fun educational activities and see how Summer Vacation can help your children do their best.

What is summer learning loss?

If they do not practice, children lose, on average, more than two-and-a-half months of what they learned in the previous school year—mainly math skills. That's one day of schoolwork for every weekday of vacation.

Summer learning loss affects school year achievement

Studies have shown that the achievement gap between students with similar abilities is almost entirely due to summer learning loss. During the school year, students of different groups achieve at pretty much the same rate, but the summer months put students who don't practice at risk of falling behind. As each summer passes, they fall further and further behind their peers.

Preventing summer learning loss

While many of the causes for summer learning loss are well known, researchers believe that a fundamental cause is lack of educational materials in the home. The best solution is to keep a child learning over the summer through rich, motivating, and effective educational activities.

Sources:

Alexander, K.L., & Entwisle, D.R. (1996). "Schools and children at risk." A. Booth, & J.F. Dunn (Eds.). Family-school links: How do they affect educational outcomes? (pp. 67-89). Mahwah, NJ: Erlbaum.

Cooper, H., Charlton, K., Valentine, J. C., & Muhlenbruck, L. (2000). "Making the most of summer school: A meta-analytic and narrative review." Monographs of the Society for Research in Child Development, 65(1), 1-118. EJ 630 022.

Cooper, H., Nye, B., Charlton, K., Lindsay, J., & Greathouse, S. (1996). "The effects of summer vacation on achievement test scores: A narrative and meta-analytic review." Review of Educational Research, 66, 227-268.

Kerry, T. and Davies, B. (1998). "Summer learning loss: the evidence and a possible solution." Support for Learning, 13, 3, 118-22.

SUMMER VACATION®
TEACHER REVIEW PANEL

Our panel of distinguished educators was instrumental in ensuring that the Summer Vacation® program offers your child maximum educational benefit. This panel provided key ideas and feedback on all aspects of our workbook series. We welcome your feedback.

Cathy Cerveny, Baltimore, MD
Maryland Teacher of the Year, 1996
Fifth-grade teacher; Integrated
Language Arts curriculum writer
Served on Maryland's Professional
Standards and Teacher Education Board

Shulamit Raz, Los Gatos, CA
Diller Award for Excellence in
Jewish Education
Resource Teacher and Mentor Teacher
ESL teacher multi-grades
Kindergarten teacher

Laurie Sybert, Lake Ozark, MO
Missouri Teacher of the Year, 1999
Second-grade teacher
Elementary Science coordinator
Fulbright Teacher Scholar

Becky Miller, Mason, OH
Gifted Coordinator for Mason City Schools
Taught elementary grades 3 and 4
Adjunct Professor at
Xavier University

Melodie Rosenfeld, Pittsburgh, CA
2nd and 3rd grade teacher
State Model Magnet Program
Elementary Education Instructor
at a teacher's college

Gemma Hoskins, Bel Air, MD
Maryland Teacher of the Year, 1992
Technology Coordinator for school
Former fifth-grade teacher and
elementary teacher specialist

Charles Mercer, Washington, DC
District of Columbia Teacher of the Year, 1999
Worked at NASA's Education Program Office
Elementary Science resource
teacher, PK–6

Rita Bailey, Brantford, ON
Elementary School Principal
Former grade 1-8 teacher
Literacy Pilot Project School

Getting ready for SIXTH GRADE!

The fifth grade was a time for your child to embrace his or her growing independence, responsibility, and individuality. Seeking ways of satisfying the need to understand the hows and whys of the world, your fifth grader probably started turning more toward friends and peer groups than to parents or caregivers. Your fifth-grade graduate may be able to:

- use synonyms, antonyms, homophones, and analogies to build vocabulary.
- recognize and apply all parts of speech.
- appreciate different forms of literature.
- incorporate suspense, dialogue, and figurative language into writing.
- edit writing from knowledge of spelling, punctuation, and grammar and usage.
- form analogies, similes, and metaphors to establish relationships.
- use deductive reasoning to make predictions and inferences in literature.
- expand personal writing in the form of letters, essays, and journal entries.
- condense learning material through note taking, outlines, and summaries.
- use and discuss symbolism and personification (attributing human characteristics to animals or objects) in writing and literature.
- identify, measure, and convert units of length, capacity, and mass in customary and metric units.
- perform operations accurately using whole numbers, fractions, and decimals.
- determine the perimeter of polygons and the area of squares and rectangles.

Monday

Activity 1

Skill: Simple Sentences

Fill in the empty blocks to make simple sentences. The sentences run across, down and diagonally.

Trekk's	Cousin	archeologst
home	Terra	an	
Trekk's	dad	is	a	writter .
mother	from	in	
Terra's		new mexico.		new york.

Math Maze

Find 49,016

- Starting with the number "5" on the left-hand side, you may proceed up, down or horizontally (sideways). The object is to end up with a total of 49,016.

- Each time you cross a "diamond" you must multiply your number by "6." Then add the number in the next circle to your total.

- The last circled number you add to your total should be the "8" in the middle.

- Remember, the numbers in the circle are meant to be added to your total, the "diamonds" mean you multiply by "6."

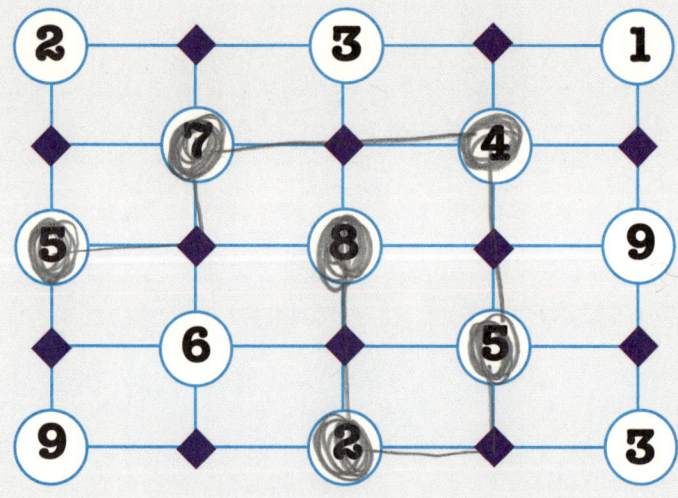

For example:

5 ◆ 4 = 34 (5 x 6 = 30 + 4 = 34)

Word Games

Can you figure out which word doesn't belong? Circle the correct answer.

1. cotton   (nylon)   silk   wool

2. canine   incisor   (dendrite)   molar

3. bear   (robin)   bat   snake

WHAT ARE YOU AFRAID OF?

Match the phobias to their correct definitions.
If you need help, use an encyclopedia or the Internet.

1. hydrophobia

a. fear of beards

2. bibliophobia

b. fear of spiders

3. pogonophobia

c. fear of the sun

4. taphophobia

d. fear of shadows

5. sciophobia

e. fear of books

6. heliophobia

f. fear of water

7. graphophobia

g. fear of graves

8. arachnophobia

h. fear of writing

FLIP OUT!

Trekk, Terra, and Dad picked up some cherries at an orchard near Lake Michigan. As they ate, Terra found two cherries on the same stem. "Look, this one is double!" she said. Dad looked at it and explained, "It has bilateral symmetry. If you draw a line down the middle, each part has the same size and shape. Things can be symmetrical along a center point, too. If you were to rotate the letter Z around its center, it would look the same. That's called rotational symmetry."

Look at the pictures below. Write down whether the shape is symmetrical. If it is, write down what kind of symmetry it has. Some things will have both bilateral and rotational symmetry.

		Symmetrical? (Yes or no)	Type? (bilateral, rotational, or both)
1.		yes	Both
2.	N	yes	rotational
3.		yes	Bilateral
4.		no	
5.		yes	Bilateral
6.	F	no	
7.		yes	Bilateral
8.		no	

Mega Math

Use pennies, nickels, dimes, quarters, half dollars, and silver dollars to solve these problems.

Tom has saved enough money to buy his favorite CD. The CD costs $9.90. He has an equal number of four different coins. Which four coins does he have? How many of each coin does he have?

Place Values

Hundred Billions 100,000,000,000s	Ten Billions 10,000,000,000s	Billions 1,000,000,000s	Hundred Millions 100,000,000s	Ten Millions 10,000,000s	Millions 1,000,000s
Hundred Thousands 100,000s	Ten Thousands 10,000s	Thousands 1,000s	Hundreds 100s	Tens 10s	Ones 1s

Write out each number in expanded notation.

Example: 99,286,611,357

90,000,000,000 + 9,000,000,000 + 200,000,000 + 80,000,000 + 6,000,000 + 600,000 + 10,000 + 1,000 + 300 + 50 + 7

1. 65,444,299

   6 000000 + 5000000 + 400000 + 40000 + 4000 + 200 + 90 + 9

2. 1,967,822

   1000000 + 900000 + 60000 + 7000 + 800 + 20 + 2

3. 479,586,286,533

   400000000000 + 70000000000 + 9 000000000 + 5 00000000 + 80000000 + 6000000 + 200000 + 80000 + 5000 + 300 + 30

4. 831,481,915

   _____

Thursday

Balance the Checking Account

Calculate the weekly balances for the checking account. Deposits add money to the account, so you must add the amount. Withdrawals take money out, so you must subtract.

Date	Deposit	Withdrawal	Balance
Jan. 2nd	$208.00		$675.00
Jan. 9th		$88.11	
Jan. 16th		$256.62	
Jan. 23rd	$1,211.47		
Jan. 30th		$118.98	
Feb. 6th	$526.50		
Feb. 13th		$733.69	
Feb. 20th	$64.99		
Feb. 27th		$412.53	
March 6th	$75.75		
March 13th		$67.88	
March 20th	$298.98		

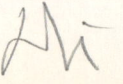

Capital Events

Terra is reading up on Henry Hudson, but the timeline below is missing capital letters and punctuation marks. **Rewrite each of the events on the timeline using complete sentences. Don't forget to include the capital letters and punctuation marks.** Remember, the first word of a sentence and *proper nouns* need to be capitalized. A *proper noun* is a noun that names a specific person, place or thing.

1607	1609	1610	1611	Today
henry hudson was commissioned by the muscovoy company to find a faster way to asia from england	henry hudson was given a ship named half moon by the dutch east india company	henry hudson thought he had entered the pacific ocean but it was actually a very large bay	the ships crew mutinied and cast hudson and his son adrift in a small boat in what is now hudson bay	the bay he entered is now known as hudson bay a strait and a river are also named after him

1607	1609	1610	1611	Today
harrey hudson was truing to find a faster way to Asia. From England.	Henry was given a ship			

Find out all about Henry Hudson at PBS Learning Adventures:
http://www.pbs.org/wnet/newyork/laic/episode1/topic1/e1_t1_s1-hh.html

11

Friday

If you could live for 500 years, would you? Why or why not? What type of things can you imagine seeing? What events can you imagine experiencing? What would the future hold?

If I was given an option to live for 500 years I would say yes. I would say yes because I would love to see what the world was like when I was borin and then 500 years later.

Trekk's Trekkin'

Terra is very impressed with Trekk's skateboard jumping, but she was curious how far he had jumped in total this day. Trekk showed her his chart listing all his jumps detailed to the nearest centimeter. "I can't add all those numbers," Terra said. "It'll take forever." "Then just round them to the nearest tenth," Trekk said. "That'll give us a general idea."

Round each number to the nearest tenth and then add them.

0.728 meters _____	0.291 meters _____
0.490 meters _____	0.969 meters _____
0.212 meters _____	0.374 meters _____
0.938 meters _____	0.555 meters _____
0.659 meters _____	0.445 meters _____
Total: _____	

"I don't think that's accurate," said Trekk, "I got more air than that!"
"Then just round them to the nearest hundredth," Terra said.

Round each number to the nearest hundredth and then add them.

0.728 meters _____	0.291 meters _____
0.490 meters _____	0.969 meters _____
0.212 meters _____	0.374 meters _____
0.938 meters _____	0.555 meters _____
0.659 meters _____	0.445 meters _____
Total: _____	

"Yo! It went down!" cried Trekk!
"Okay, I warned you. We'll do it your way," responded Terra.

Now add them without rounding.

0.728 meters	0.291 meters
0.490 meters	0.969 meters
0.212 meters	0.374 meters
0.938 meters	0.555 meters
0.659 meters	0.445 meters
Total: _____	

"Aaargh!" said Trekk. "From now on I round up everything!"

Northern Lights

Image courtesy of NASA Aurora Gallery, © Todd & Brenda Throop

Sometimes called aurora borealis, the northern lights begin with the sun. When the sun flares, solar particles burst away into deep space and fly toward earth. When they get close enough, the particles are caught in the earth's magnetic field. The particles then give off light particles, (or photons), when they smash into the gases in our atmosphere, often in a variety of colors.

In times past, people created myths to explain the northern lights. The Vikings thought they were the reflections of dead maidens. The Inuit believed that when the lights changed rapidly, dead friends were trying to contact their living relatives. The Danish said the lights were reflections of the flapping wings of swans that flew so far to the north that they were caught in the ice.

Using what you know about the science behind the northern lights, write your own myth about how and why they happen. A myth explains natural events like the northern lights by using a story rather than science.

_____
_____
_____
_____
_____
_____
_____
_____
_____
_____
_____
_____
_____
_____

Star Light, Far Light!

Trekk, who loves astronomy, told Terra that stars are so far away, their distances are measured in **LIGHT YEARS**—the distance light travels in one year—about 5,869,200,000,000 miles, or 9,445,561,000,000 km. "Scientists can be very exact about measuring," Trekk said, pointing out stars. "That one is 7.392 light years away, while that star is 4.287 light years away, and…" "Wait a minute!" Terra interrupted. "Those numbers are too complicated. Couldn't we just round them?"

Round these star distances to the nearest hundredth:

1) Tau Ceti   11.412 _____
2) Proxima Centauri   4.235 _____
3) Epsilon Indi   11.249 _____
4) Sirius B   8.673 _____
5) Barnard's Star   5.969 _____
6) L 789-6   11.124 _____
7) 61 Cygnus A   11.215 _____
8) UV Ceti B   8.548 _____
9) GQ Andromedae   11.220 _____
10) Alpha Centauri A   4.336 _____

Round these star distances to the nearest tenth:

11) 61 Cygnus B   11.215 _____
12) UV Ceti A   8.552 _____
13) Sirius A   8.667 _____
14) Alpha Centauri B   4.339 _____
15) Ross 248   10.396 _____
16) HD 173739   11.254 _____
17) Wolf 359   7.804 _____
18) Epsilon Eridani   10.631 _____
19) Lalande 21185   8.190 _____
20) Ross 154   9.523 _____

Stellar distances are also measured in PARSECS. 1 parsec is equal to 3.26 light years. Convert the rounded numbers above to parsecs by multiplying by 3.26.

1) _____
2) _____
3) _____
4) _____
5) _____
6) _____
7) _____
8) _____
9) _____
10) _____

11) _____
12) _____
13) _____
14) _____
15) _____
16) _____
17) _____
18) _____
19) _____
20) _____

More Mega Math

Each of the symbols represents a number between 1 - 10. Can you figure out which number should fill in the blank?

 = _____

Fractions, Decimals & Percentages

Example: $\dfrac{15}{100}$ = .15 = 15%

Fill in the blanks below.

1 $\dfrac{1}{100}$ = .____ = ____%

2 ____ = .13 = ____%

3 ____ = .____ = 66%

4 $\dfrac{77}{100}$ = .____ = ____%

5 ____ = .____ = 98%

6 $\dfrac{33}{100}$ = .____ = ____%

7 ____ = .32 = ____%

8 $\dfrac{42}{100}$ = .____ = ____%

Similes, Metaphors and Personification

Simile: compares two things using the word like or as.

Metaphor: compares two things without using the word like or as.

Personification: compares two things by giving human qualities to things that are not human.

A. simile   B. metaphor   C. personification
Label each sentence as A, B or C.

1 He ran as fast as a cougar.   _____A_____

2 The waves crashed like thunder.   _____A_____

3 The lion's mane was a wreath of fur.   _____

4 The rain danced across the schoolyard.   _____

5 The sleeping snake could have been mistaken for a coil of rope.   _____

6 Her face was as white as a ghost.   _____A_____

7 Twilight tiptoed into the daylight.   _____

8 The dandelions on the lawn appeared to be green and yellow carpeting.   _____

Hudson's Children

CHAPTER TWO

Terra headed to the baggage claim area of the Detroit Metro Airport to meet Trekk and his dad. She saw Trekk before he saw her. She looked at Trekk the same way she did every summer when they first saw each other—trying to see what was different. Terra noticed that he was taller than she expected, and what on earth was he doing to his hair? She could see that he was looking at her in the same deliberate way as he and his dad got closer to where she stood waiting.

"Hey," she said to Trekk. "Hi, Uncle Phil."

"Hi, Terra," Trekk's dad said. "How was your flight?"

"Good, really. I'm pretty used to it now." At first, when Terra had flown alone it had seemed scary, like rowing across a lake when you couldn't see the other side. The flight attendants were always nice to her, and she was comfortable now. Trekk had felt the same way when it was his turn to go West, and it was one of the things they always talked about.

Uncle Phil looked different to Terra, too, and she said so to Trekk later as they loaded their camping equipment. Trekk's dad had borrowed a truck and gear from an old college friend in Michigan, which is why Terra had met her uncle and cousin there. "It's not been a great year in the city," Trekk said, "and I think Dad's just tired. I don't think he had to come out here. I think he just wanted to. Where do you suppose these could fit?" he said, as he waggled a pair of canoe paddles.

They set off the next morning, and Terra marveled at the green countryside in this part of the country. They went northwest at first, to the west edge of the state along Lake Michigan, up past the apple and cherry orchards. They camped the first night in a town called White Cloud. As soon as their tents were raised and a fire built, Terra and Trekk went for a moonlight hike. The night air smelled of campfires and pine, and Terra felt as though she were moving back in time as well as away from town.

"I love it, the smell of it, as if you were breathing in the whole world at its best," Terra announced with a relaxed sigh.

"I do, too," Trekk said. "But just wait until tomorrow. We're going sailing."

Monday

Activity 2

Skill: Reading Comprehension

1. How did Trekk look different to Terra as she left the airplane?

   _____

   _____

2. How have Terra's feelings about flying alone changed?

   _____

   _____

3. Why did the three meet in Michigan?

   _____

   _____

4. Which direction did they go when they began to travel?

   _____

5. What crops did they observe?

   _____

6. What do Terra, Trekk and Trekk's dad do in White Cloud, Michigan?

   _____

7. What does the group plan to do the next day?

   _____

Odd Number Out

Can you figure out which number doesn't belong?
Circle the correct answer.

1. 24   72   108   63   12

2. 33   132   71   66   11

3. 56   14   28   92   98

Adverbial Phrases

An adverbial phrase is a group of words that acts as an adverb.
They tell where, when, how or to what extent.

Example: The boat sped (along the river.)

Circle the adverbial phrases in the sentences below.

1. She ate her hamburger in a hurry.

2. He lost his watch in the back yard.

3. You better run as fast as you can.

4. My uncle works nights and sleeps during the day.

5. My brother ran on the treadmill for an hour.

6. The mechanic tuned the car with precision.

HEY OLD SPORT!

Match the terms with their sport.
If you need help, use an encyclopedia or the Internet.

1. balk

2. fair catch

3. two-line pass

4. takedown

5. dismount

6. fault

7. over and back

8. hazard

a. basketball

b. golf

c. football

d. tennis

e. baseball

f. hockey

g. gymnastics

h. wrestling

Angles

Right angles measure 90°

Acute angles measure less than 90°

Obtuse angles measure more than 90°

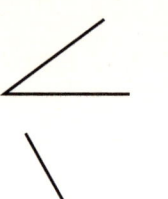

Identify each type of angle and circle the correct answer.

①

45°

Right **Acute** Obtuse

②

180°

Right Acute **Obtuse**

③

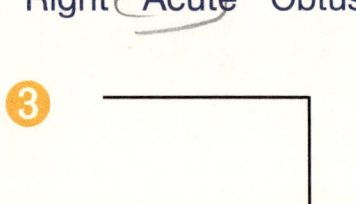

90°

Right Acute Obtuse

④

70°

Right **Acute** Obtuse

⑤

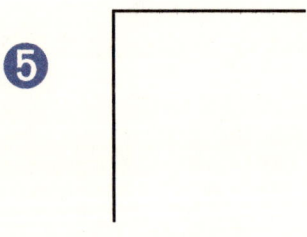

90°

Right Acute Obtuse

⑥

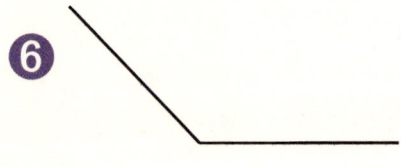

120°

Right Acute **Obtuse**

Mega Math

Can you solve the following problem? Assign different values for consonants and vowels. Can you detect a rule for solving the unknown amount?

Jamal went to the store and bought groceries for dinner. He bought the following items:

- Hamburger $3.60
- Buns $1.30
- Potato Chips   ?

How much did the potato chips cost?
What's the rule?

Punctuation & Capitalization Quiz

Punctuate and capitalize the paragraph below:

sara couldn't wait for summer vacation to begin her

family was planning a trip to europe mom when are we

leaving for our trip asked sara we will leave on june 30

answered sara's mother

Thursday

Parts of the Whole System!

By dividing the numerator (top number) of a fraction by the denominator (bottom number), fractions can be changed into decimals.

$$\frac{7}{8}$$

$$8 \overline{)7.0} \quad \begin{array}{r} .875 \\ \hline \end{array}$$
$$60$$
$$40$$

Convert these fractions to decimals using division. (If the division problem keeps going, round it to the nearest thousandth, as you learned on page 15!)

1 $\dfrac{1}{5}$ **2** $\dfrac{3}{4}$ **3** $\dfrac{7}{10}$ **4** $\dfrac{3}{8}$ **5** $\dfrac{6}{15}$ **6** $\dfrac{7}{12}$

7 $\dfrac{4}{4}$ **8** $\dfrac{1}{13}$ **9** $\dfrac{4}{9}$ **10** $\dfrac{2}{7}$ **11** $\dfrac{14}{15}$ **12** $\dfrac{8}{9}$

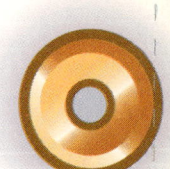

13 $\dfrac{5}{11}$ **14** $\dfrac{7}{9}$ **15** $\dfrac{8}{13}$ **16** $\dfrac{3}{19}$ **17** $\dfrac{15}{17}$ **18** $\dfrac{21}{28}$

Trekk has been apprenticed to a master printer. Unfortunately, he forgot to include punctuation marks. Help Trekk place the correct punctuation marks and capital letters in each sentence. Using the correct punctuation, rewrite the news story on the lines below.

canadas worst train disaster

on june 29 1867 a special passenger train plunged into the richlieu river near beloil killing 97 german immigrants and 2 train conductors the train headed toward montreal on the grand trunk railway and went through a drawbridge left open for the passage of barges on the river below rescuers from montreal and local residents worked day and night to recover victims

curious crowds gathered at the scene of the accident contributing to a tense atmosphere imprison the mechanic its his fault shouted one local woman

i know people want answers but its too early to make judgments at this time said one coroner the investigation will continue over the next few weeks

_____

_____

_____

_____

_____

_____

_____

Friday

You are a superhero and it is your job to fight crime. However, it is up to you to create which superpowers you will have and what you are capable of doing. Using this page, describe your superpowers (how they work, what they do) and what kind of situations you will use them in. You can even write your own adventure!

_____
_____
_____
_____
_____
_____
_____
_____
_____
_____
_____
_____
_____
_____

Comparing Apples to Apples!

Near the town of White Cloud, Terra, Trekk and his father visited an apple orchard, where they collected a whole bucket of apples. Later, when they were munching on a few, Trekk's father decided to have a little fun with a little puzzle.

He cut a red apple into 3 pieces, then he cut a green one into 6 pieces.

"Which is more—two pieces of the red, or three pieces of the green one?" he asked.

The kids had to think about it...

Compare other fractions. Decide which is larger. If you need to, determine which is larger by dividing the numerator by the denominator as you learned on page 24.

1 1/4 and 3/8

2 2/5 and 1/3

3 4/6 and 4/10

4 5/8 and 2/3

5 1/2 and 5/8

6 7/9 and 4/5

7 7/8 and 13/15

8 9/10 and 19/21

9 2/11 and 4/23

10 5/100 and 7/125

11 .65 and 4/6

12 5/8 and .60

13 7/9 and .75

14 .20 and 2/11

15 7/125 and .8

Ecosystems

An ecosystem is an interconnected habitat, where different living things play different roles to help the whole community thrive. While scientists look at many different features—weather, animals, the impact of humans—ecosystems are usually grouped according to land features.

What ecosystem do you live in? Survey the local land, climate, plant, and animal patterns in your area.

1. Describe the climate in your area. Does it have 4 distinct seasons? Is it rainy or dry?

2. Describe the land in your area. Is it flat, rolling, or mountainous? Is it near the ocean?

3. Describe the plants in your area. Is it mainly grassland, or do trees and shrubs grow there?

4. Describe the way people use the land. Do they primarily hunt, farm, mine minerals, or work in factories?

5. Using the chart above, which ecosystem most accurately describes where you live?

6. Look at the ecosystems in the chart. What animal might you find living in each?

7. How might people use the land in each ecosystem?

Who's Who in an Ecosystem?

While differences exist among ecosystems, all have some common features. In any ecosystem, producers, consumers and decomposers play a role. Producers create necessary resources in an ecosystem. Consumers make use of those resources. Decomposers break down useless material so it can be reused. The proportion of producers, consumers and decomposers differs in each ecosystem.

Study the pie chart for this ecosystem, then answer the questions:

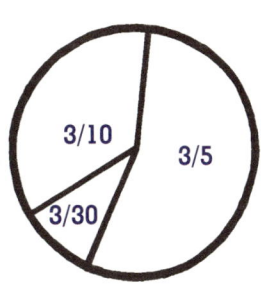

3/5 — Consumers
3/10 — Producers
3/30 — Decomposers

1.) Write the decimal number for the number of consumers:

_____

2.) Write the decimal number for the number of producers:

_____

3.) Write the decimal number for the number of decomposers: _____

4.) What is the combined number of producers and decomposers (both in decimal form and in fraction form)? _____

5.) What is the combined number of producers and consumers (both in decimal form and in fraction form)? _____

6.) If the number of consumers was cut by half, and that half was split equally between the producers and decomposers, what portion would there then be of each category? _____

7.) If the number of decomposers is cut in half, with the half being split equally between the other two groups, what would the new totals be? _____

Discover ecosystems with other kids at the Missouri Botanical Garden!
http://mbgnet.mobot.org

Grid Logic

For examples on how to complete Grid Logic, read the instructions at the back of the book.

	Nathan	Tino	Vanessa	Azra	Maple	Oak	Birch	Spruce
Kamali								
Rodriguez								
Bahaligia								
Feinstein								
Maple								
Oak								
Birch								
Spruce								

Mrs. Osaki's fifth grade class is doing a science project on trees. Azra and her three friends each were allowed to choose a tree to study. Based on the clues below, can you determine each child's first and last name and the tree that they studied?

1 Nathan, the child who studied the oak tree, and the Bahaligia boy all lived in the same neighborhood.

2 Vanessa, the child who studied the maple tree, and the Kamali child often ate lunch together.

3 The Rodriguez girl studied a tree that was a conifer, while all the other children studied deciduous trees.

4 By researching his science project, Tino found that he was studying a tree with white, paper-like bark that peels easily, while the Feinstein boy found that his type of tree is capable of producing edible syrup.

Prefixes

Prefixes are added to the beginning of base words. Add a prefix to each word below and then write a sentence using the new word.

Prefixes: mis, dis, re, un, non, pre
Base Words: appear, understand, view, read, sure, stop

1 _____dis_ appear _____

_____

2 _____mis_ understand _____

_____

3 _____pre_ view _____

_____

4 _____mis_ read _____

_____

5 _____un_ sure _____

_____

6 _____ stop _____

_____

_____

Hudson's Children

CHAPTER THREE

Trekk, his dad, and Terra drove early the next morning to Petoskey, a city on Lake Michigan. There, Trekk's dad had arranged a one-day sailing class in small, single-person sailboats called Optimist Dinghies.

Trekk was impatient, though, as the instructor, Mr. Guindon, explained the parts of a boat and how they worked. His impatience grew when he noticed the boats dancing on the waves in the harbor. Trekk's attention returned when the instructor talked about how to sail the dinghy. Mr. Guindon explained some important sailing terms—sailing with the wind; tacking or moving into the wind; and the fastest way, sailing across the wind. "Always let the wind lead you," he said. "If it shifts, you must be ready."

Mr. Guindon helped them rig their boats, attaching the bottom bar, or boom, to the foot of the sail, and then hoisting the sail. At last, they untied the lines and moved away from the dock. "All right," shouted Trekk as the breeze picked up and his dinghy began to move. Suddenly, his boat was "luffing," or stalling, because the wind had changed direction. With some wild motions of the boom and the rudder, Trekk got moving again.

Fumbling at first, everyone soon began to get better at controlling the boats. Terra loved it, feeling as if she were partners with the breeze. Trekk happily coached himself aloud, and his dad smiled, looking relaxed. Suddenly the wind increased. Terra sensed it instantly, and adjusted her rudder and sail to catch it. The boat skipped ahead. Trekk caught it too, and extended his sail as far as he could. He was sailing across the wind, and the dinghy rapidly picked up speed. "Yahoooooo!" he shouted, rising.

"Trekk, don't stand," Dad called, but Trekk was too far away to hear, and took a skateboarder's pose as the dinghy bounced through the water. At that moment the boat hit a wave hard. Losing his balance, Trekk leaned on the rudder and the boat spun. The sail shot across the boat, swinging the boom like a baseball bat. The boom cracked Trekk hard in the knees, and his dinghy turned over.

Underwater, Trekk was stunned by the cold and the swiftness of what had happened. He bobbed to the surface quickly, grateful for his life jacket.

Mr. Guindon, in a small motorboat, reached him first and fished him out. Although Mr. Guindon said that this could have happened to anyone, Trekk felt foolish. Not everyone, he admitted to himself, pretends to be skateboarding.

That evening, as Trekk sat rubbing his sore knees, Terra sat down and grinned, "I guess that's why they call it a boom, huh?"

"Funny," Trekk said.

Monday

Activity 3

Skill: Clarifying

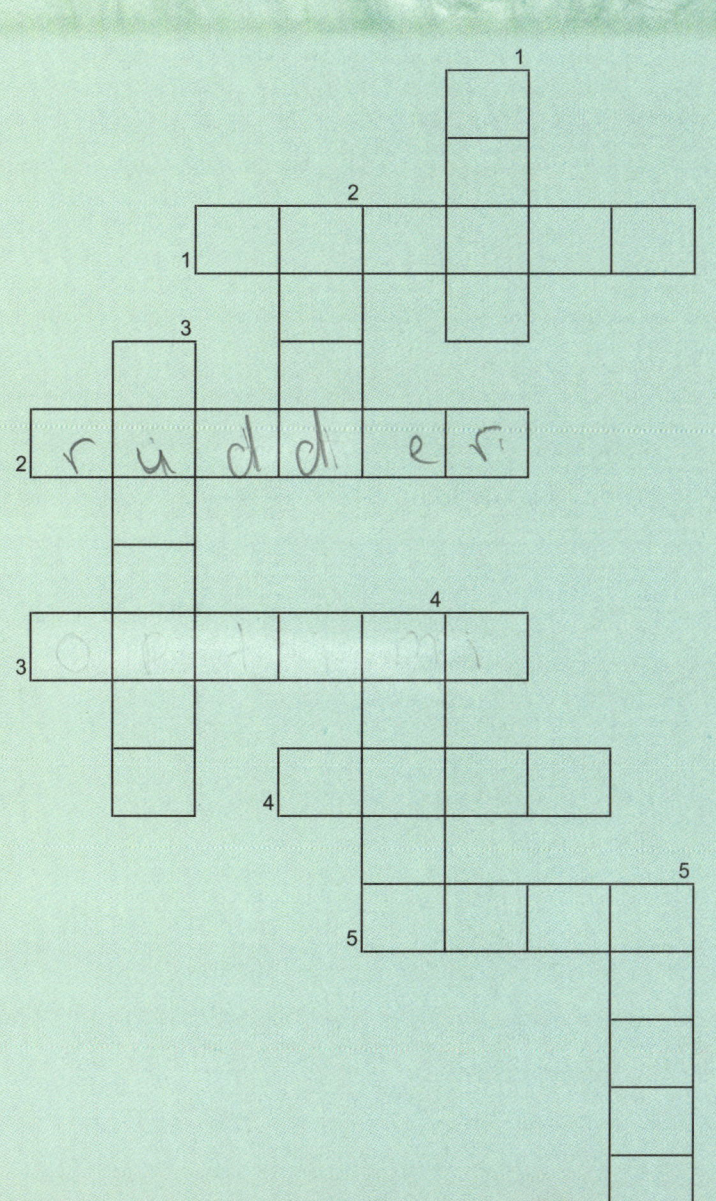

r u d d e r

o p _ _ _ _

Across

1. Sailing _____ the wind is fastest.

2. Used to steer a sailboat

3. The type of sailboat Terra and Trekk sailed

4. What moves a sailing vessel

5. To move a sailboat into the wind

Down

1. What swept across the deck when the wind changed

2. How the water felt when Trekk fell

3. Stalling a sailboat by going directly into the wind

4. To raise a sail

5. Where Trekk was struck

Math Maze

Race for 350!

- Starting at the top with the number "48" and ending with the number "31," choose the correct path down to the bottom that will result in 350.

- Each time you cross a "triangle" you must subtract three from your number. The circled numbers are to be added—no subtraction or multiplication.

- You must stay on the lines to reach the 350 figure.

- Remember, each triangle is worth -3.

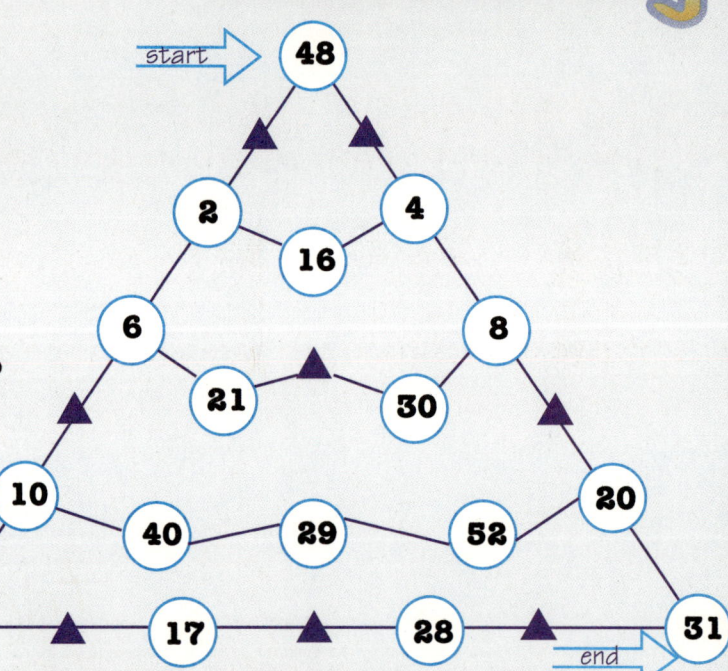

For example:
8 ▲ 20 = 25 (8 - 3 = 5 + 20 = 25)

Word Games

Can you figure out which word doesn't belong?

1 carp   swordfish   shark   red snapper

2 goat   sheep   cow   pig

3 peach   banana   avocado   cherry

IT'S ALL GREEK TO ME

Match the Latin names to the animal.
If you need help, use an encyclopedia or the Internet.

1. Felis catus

2. Panthera leo

3. Canis familiaris

4. Equus caballus

5. Orycteropus afer

6. Carassius auratus

7. Orcinus orca

8. Homo sapiens

a. dog

b. horse

c. aardvark

d. cat

e. human

f. lion

g. goldfish

h. killer whale

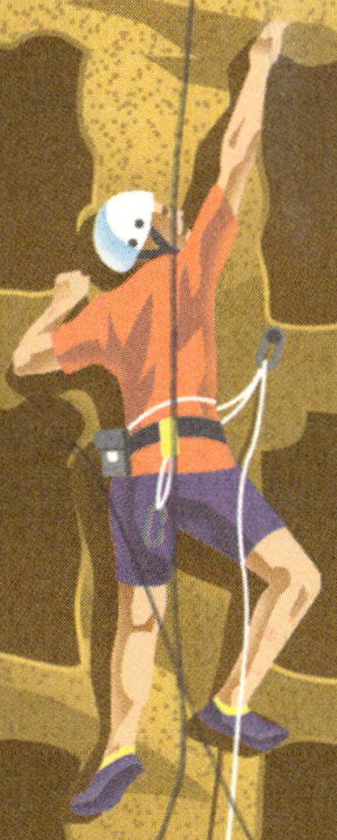

ANGLE TANGLE

Measure the angles below using a protractor. Then decide what kind of angle it is. For help using a protractor, see the last page in the book.

1.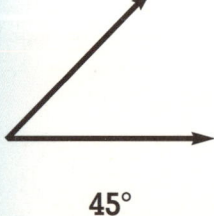

45°

acute

2.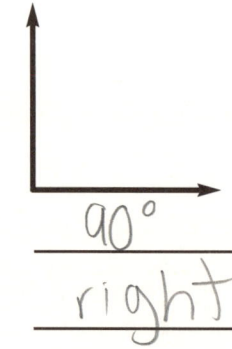

90°

right

Acute
(less than 90 degrees)

Right
(exactly 90 degrees)

Obtuse
(greater than 90 degrees)

3.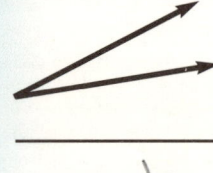

acute

4.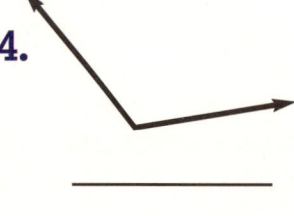

5.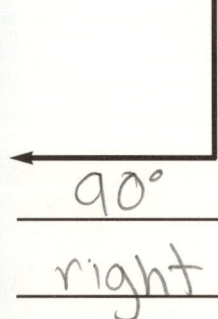

90°

right

6.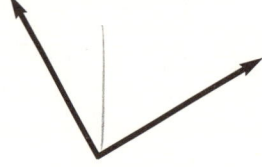

obtuse

7.

obtuse

8.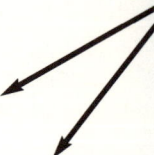

acute

9.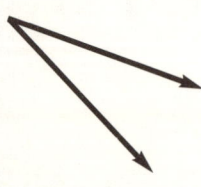

acute

10.

obtuee

11.

acute

12.

90°

right

Mega Math

Use pennies, nickels, dimes, quarters, half dollars, and silver dollars to solve these problems.

Jennifer wants to buy a new pair of blue jeans. The jeans she picked out cost $19.00. She has the exact amount. She has an even number of 5 separate coins. Which five coins is she going to pay with? How many of each?

Multiplication of Fractions

When multipying fractions, multiply across, then reduce the fraction. Match each equation to the correct missing number.

Example: $\dfrac{3}{4} \times \dfrac{2}{9} = \dfrac{6}{36} = \dfrac{1}{6}$

1 $\dfrac{2}{3} \times \dfrac{3}{3} = \dfrac{2}{\underline{}}$

2 $\dfrac{8}{5} \times \dfrac{5}{\underline{}} = 1$

3 $\dfrac{7}{8} \times \dfrac{4}{5} = \dfrac{\underline{}}{10}$

4 $\dfrac{3}{\underline{}} \times \dfrac{7}{9} = \dfrac{7}{18}$

5 $\dfrac{6}{7} \times \dfrac{2}{6} = \dfrac{\underline{}}{7}$

6 $\dfrac{5}{9} \times \dfrac{1}{5} = \dfrac{1}{\underline{}}$

a 8

b 9

c 2

d 6

e 3

f 7

Thursday

Plot the Coordinates

Plot the coordinates on the graph below and label them with the correct letters. The first number tells the horizontal position (how far to the right). The second number tells the vertical position (how far up). The first one is done for you.

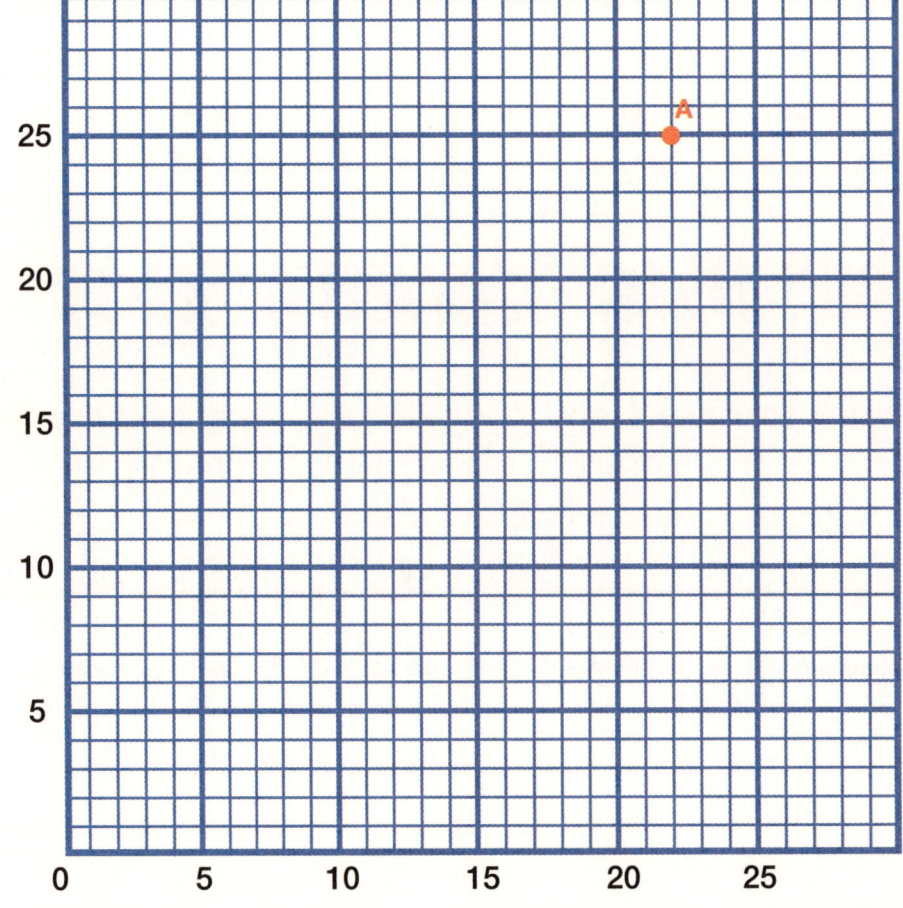

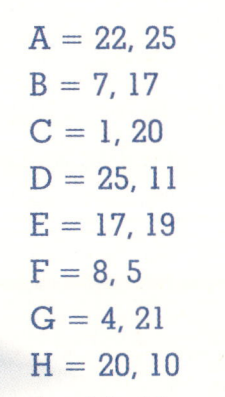

A = 22, 25
B = 7, 17
C = 1, 20
D = 25, 11
E = 17, 19
F = 8, 5
G = 4, 21
H = 20, 10
I = 10, 20

J = 14, 19
K = 4, 9
L = 24, 19
M = 2, 8
N = 9, 7
O = 13, 13
P = 12, 15
Q = 16, 23
R = 22, 2

S = 3, 18
T = 10, 10
U = 11, 22
V = 13, 17
W = 8, 8
X = 9, 12
Y = 11, 25
Z = 20, 24

Pricey Pronouns

"Trade you for a candy bar," Dad offered.

"You ate the last one," Terra said. "You can't trade something that isn't there!"

Dad smiled slyly, "I can so. People trade words all the time."

"Like what?" Trekk asked, rolling his eyes. "I sense another car game coming."

"You trade nouns for pronouns all the time so that you don't have to keep repeating the same noun over and over," Dad said. "Every time you use a pronoun, I'll add some change to our candy fund."

Use the pronouns from the chart in the sentences below and add up how much change you've earned for the candy fund.

Personal Pronouns	Possessive Pronouns	Reflexive Pronouns	Demonstrative Pronouns
 $0.25	 $0.50	 $1.00	This, these, that, those $0.75
I, we, he, she, it, we, you, they, me, her, him, it, us, them	Mine, yours, his, hers, its, ours, theirs	Myself, yourself, himself, itself, ourselves, yourselves, themselves	

1. Trekk was distracted as _____ instructor talked about _____ parts of the boat. $_____

2. Trekk fell into the water after _____ pretended that _____ sailboat was a skateboard. $_____

3. _____ admitted to _____ that pretending was not a good idea. $_____

Total earned $_____

Try writing some sentences of your own with pronouns that add up to the values given.

4. $1.25 _____

_____

5. $0.75 _____

_____

6. $0.50 _____

_____

7. $1.50 _____

_____

Friday

Congratulations! You have just been elected Mayor of your city. So after all the parties, it's time to get down to business. Discuss your plan for improving the city and ways to solve various problems.

_____
_____
_____
_____
_____
_____
_____
_____
_____
_____
_____
_____
_____
_____
_____
_____
_____
_____

"Euclid Do It!"

The Euclid Method is a simple way to find the Greatest Common Factor (GCF) for two numbers. If you don't know about the Greatest Common Factor, check out the last page in this book. Here's how it works. Let's say we wanted to find the GCF for 12 and 176...

1. Divide the larger number by the smaller one.

$$176 \div 12 = 14$$
with a remainder of 8

2. Now divide the smaller number (the divisor) by that remainder.

$$12 \div 8 = 1 \text{ with a remainder of 4.}$$

3. Repeat this step until the division leaves NO REMAINDER.

$$8 \div 4 = 2$$

4. When the division leaves no remainder, then you have done it! The divisor in the last step is your GCF. (The GCF for 176 and 12 is 2.)

Now find the GCF for these numbers:

1. 166 and 12   **2.** 252 and 7   **3.** 98 and 84

4. 14 and 441   **5.** 96 and 12   **6.** 188 and 16

7. 248 and 160   **8.** 369 and 13   **9.** 245 and 14

10. 121 and 22   **11.** 24 and 246   **12.** 468 and 22

Forest Life

The Boreal Shield, stretching from Newfoundland to Alberta, is Canada's largest ecosystem. It covers 1.8 million square kilometers, or 695,000 square miles. The shield rock that lies beneath the Boreal Shield forms the heart of the North American continent and is one of the world's oldest geological formations. A billion years ago, this rock was a mountain range. Over time, as the earth changed, it shifted into an enormous plain of stone. Depressions in the rock, which were carved by the movement of glaciers, later became the many lakes, ponds, and rivers that exist throughout the area.

Over 75% of the Boreal Shield is covered by forests, with much of the remaining land consisting of exposed bedrock on which grow a variety of shrubs and lichen. There are also areas of wetland known as "peatlands." Many of Canada's animals, including beavers, lynx, moose, marten, woodland caribou, wolves, striped skunks, bobcats and black bears, live in the Boreal Shield, along with a wide variety of migratory birds.

Life in the Boreal Shield can be a challenge. Cold weather means that the growing season of plants is short, and that animals must struggle to find food in the winter. Plants and trees must adapt to highly acidic soil, which slows their growth. Frequent fires also devastate the forests, although these also renew the environment by triggering new plant growth, killing insects that damage trees, and diversifying animals' habitats.

Match the Facts

Match the item in the left column with a description in the right column.

_____ 1.	acidic soil	**a.**	well-known forest animal
_____ 2.	shield rock	**b.**	billion-year-old geological structure
_____ 3.	forest fires	**c.**	Canada's largest ecosystem
_____ 4.	lakes and ponds	**d.**	about 1.8 million square kilometers
_____ 5.	mountain range	**e.**	from depressions carved by glaciers
_____ 6.	woodland caribou	**f.**	a consequence of the cold weather
_____ 7.	short growing season	**g.**	a factor that slows plant growth
_____ 8.	Boreal Shield	**h.**	events that renew the environment
_____ 9.	peatlands	**i.**	features growth of lichen and shrubs
_____ 10.	695,000 square miles	**j.**	wetland areas
_____ 11.	glaciers	**k.**	origin of the Boreal Shield
_____ 12.	exposed bedrock	**l.**	carved into rock

Counting Moose

Terra, Trekk and his dad started seeing so many moose, they decided to have a counting contest—winner gets a stuffed toy moose.

Who won? Add up the numbers to see. Then, find the daily average for each week, and the average for each day of the week. (Remember: To find an average, add the numbers together and then divide by the <u>number</u> of <u>numbers</u>. The first ones are done!)

Trekk's Moose Count

Week	Mon	Tues	Wed	Thur	Fri	Sat	Sun	Total This Week	Daily Avg. for the Wk.
1	2	2	3	4	1	4	5	21	3
2	2	2	2	2	2	3	1		
3	4	0	2	5	3	5	2		
4	0	0	1	3	4	4	2		
Average for Each Day	2								

Terra's Moose Count

Week	Mon	Tues	Wed	Thur	Fri	Sat	Sun	Total This Week	Daily Avg. for the Wk.
1	1	2	4	0	2	2	3		
2	2	3	0	1	2	4	2		
3	3	1	4	2	5	4	2		
4	0	0	4	3	7	2	5		
Average for Each Day									

Trekk's Dad's Moose Count

Week	Mon	Tues	Wed	Thur	Fri	Sat	Sun	Total This Week	Daily Avg. for the Wk.
1	4	2	1	4	2	1	0		
2	2	2	2	4	3	4	4		
3	1	1	1	0	1	1	2		
4	5	3	2	4	6	6	2		
Average for Each Day									

More Mega Math

Each of the symbols represents a number between 1 - 10. Can you figure out which number should fill in the blank?

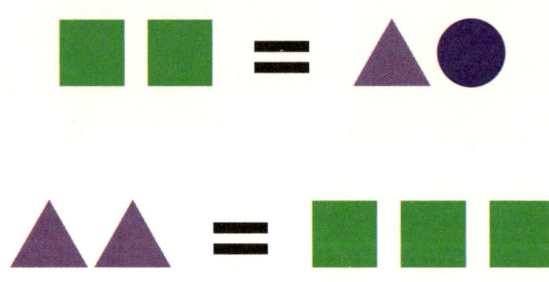

Suffixes

Suffixes are added to the end of base words. Add a suffix to each word below and then write a sentence using the new word.

Suffixes: less, able, ance, ment, ness, ly
Base Words: agree, hope, believe, happy, kind, appear

① _____

② _____

③ _____

④ _____

⑤ _____

⑥ _____

Calculating Discount Percentages

Match the correct percentages with the sale price. To find out the percentage, divide the amount saved by the total amount.

Example: Regular Price $200 $50 \div 200 = .25 = 25\%$
Save $50

1 Regular Price $100   **a** 10%
Save $15

2 Regular Price $60   **b** 30%
Save $6

3 Regular Price $48   **c** 50%
Save $19.20

4 Regular Price $90   **d** 15%
Save $27

5 Regular Price $250   **e** 40%
Save $50

6 Regular Price $782   **f** 20%
Save $391

Hudson's Children

CHAPTER FOUR

Trekk would like to have stayed in Petoskey to improve his sailing skills, but his dad was ready to move north. They quickly covered the forty miles to Mackinaw City, where Lake Huron meets Lake Michigan. "We'll cross into the Upper Peninsula here," Trekk's dad said. Trekk whistled at the size of the bridge they had to cross.

"That's some bridge," he said.

"It's five times the length of the Brooklyn Bridge. From the time it was built in the 1950s until 1998, the Mackinac Bridge was the longest suspension bridge in the world," his dad pointed out.

"Where's the longest?" Terra asked.

"Japan, I think," her uncle said. "And then one in Denmark, and then 'Mighty Mac.'" As they drove over the bridge, Trekk saw that he could look through the deck at the Straits of Mackinac two hundred feet below. The truck tires growled over the open steel grid.

"Why is it open like that?" Trekk asked.

"So the wind goes through," his dad replied. "The bridge moves in high winds, but it doesn't sway."

"You don't think about bridges moving around, do you?" Terra asked.

"I don't want to, either," said Trekk as he peered at the Straits far below.

They went on north through the Upper Peninsula past the Hiawatha National Forest. "Sault Ste. Marie, guys," Trekk's dad said as he approached the town. "Gateway to Canada." Terra noticed that her uncle was veering off course and heading toward the west of town. "You're going to the shipwreck museum, aren't you?" She grinned at the puzzled Trekk. "I looked at the map."

At the Great Lakes Shipwreck Museum, near Whitefish Point and its old lighthouse, they moved from exhibit to exhibit. The danger of the five lakes became apparent as they discovered that more than 6,000 ships and 30,000 lives had been lost. They learned about the giant Edmund Fitzgerald, which disappeared, crew and all, during a November storm. Trekk and Terra looked a long time at the bell of the doomed ship, recovered twenty years after the event, and they listened to a tape of a song about the tragedy. On the drive back to Sault Ste. Marie, Trekk shivered as he thought of his five minutes underwater when his little boat had capsized.

"On to Canada," his dad said when they arrived back in Sault Ste. Marie. He began to sing the Canadian national anthem, "O, Canada!"

"Where does he get this stuff?" Terra said, rolling her eyes.

"I think he plans it," Trekk said. "I just wish he had practiced it."

Monday

Activity 4

Skill: Verbs

Choose the correct answer for each question. Circle your choice.

1. Trekk would have liked to remain longer in Petoskey to
   a. examine the bridge more carefully.
   b. improve his sailing skills.
   c. learn more about shipwrecks.
   d. apologize to Mr. Guindon.

2. When Trekk first saw the Mackinac Bridge, he
   a. sang "O, Canada."
   b. chimed in with a poem.
   c. whistled in amazement.
   d. peered over the deck.

3. The Straits of Mackinac are where
   a. Lake Erie joins Lake Superior.
   b. Lake Huron becomes Lake Ontario.
   c. Lake Michigan empties into Lake Ontario.
   d. Lake Huron connects to Lake Michigan.

4. The Mackinac Bridge has an open deck to
   a. allow the wind to pass through.
   b. permit large freighters to pass below it.
   c. create openings for viewing the Straits below.
   d. encourage walkers to use the bridge.

5. After they crossed the Mackinac Bridge, the travelers
   a. headed west to Whitefish Point.
   b. studied the map of Canada.
   c. toured the town of St. Ignace.
   d. went north through the Upper Peninsula.

6. The freighter Edmund Fitzgerald
   a. was converted into a museum.
   b. grounded on Whitefish Point.
   c. disappeared during a storm.
   d. survived a furious storm.

Odd Number Out

Can you figure out which number doesn't belong?
Circle the correct answer.

①	36	20	16	9	64
②	25	4	49	42	36
③	1	16	64	81	56

Comparative and Superlative

Most comparative forms of adjectives end in "er." Most superlative forms of adjectives end in "est." Fill in the blanks below. The first one is done for you.

	Word	Comparative	Superlative
①	large	larger	largest
②	high	higher	highest
③	big	biger	bigest
④	quick	quicker	quickest
⑤	long	longer	longest
⑥	fast	faster	fastest

COUNTRY CURRENCIES

Match the currencies with their countries.
If you need help, use an encyclopedia or the Internet.

1. Brazil

2. China

3. Mexico

4. India

5. Israel

6. Russia

7. South Africa

8. Japan

a. yen

b. rand

c. réal

d. yuan

e. peso

f. shekel

g. rupee

h. rouble

Finding Area

Find the area for each shape.

Rectangle Area = length x width

Triangle Area = $\frac{1}{2}$ x base x height

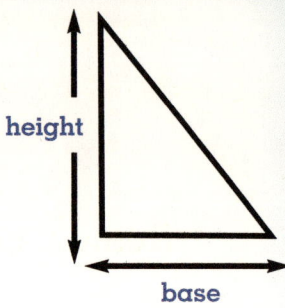
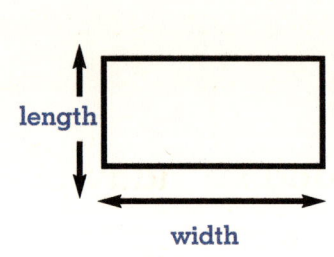
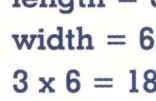

height

length

width

base

length = 3
width = 6
3 x 6 = 18

base = 3
height = 4
$\frac{1}{2}$ x 3 x 4 = 6

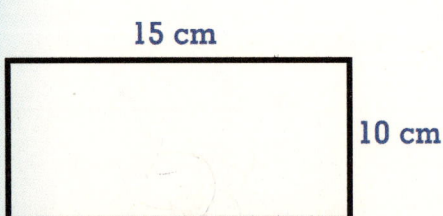

15 cm

10 cm

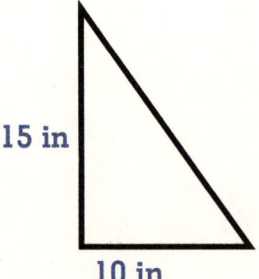

15 in

10 in

1. Area = __150__ centimeters

2. Area = __150__ inches

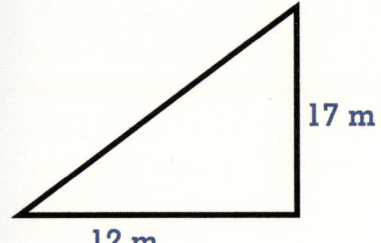

17 m

12 m

19.8 mm

17.4 mm

3. Area = __140__ meters

4. Area _____ millimeters

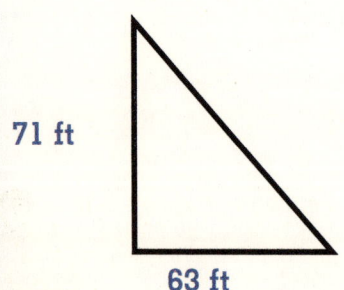

71 ft

63 ft

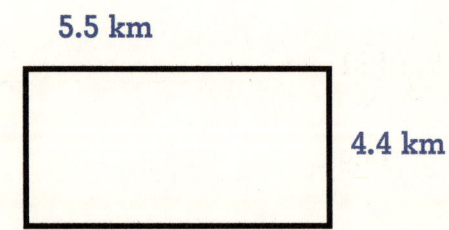

5.5 km

4.4 km

5. Area = _____ feet

6. Area = _____ kilometers

Mega Math

Can you solve the following problem? Assign different values for consonants and vowels. Can you detect a rule for solving the unknown amount?

Keshia needed birthday party supplies. She bought:

- Balloons $4.75

- Candles $4.00

- Favors   ?

How much did the favors cost? What's the rule?

Find the Percent of Each Number

Convert each percent to a decimal, then multiply to solve the problems below.

Example: 6% of 32 = .06 x 32 = 1.92

1 5% of 25   = _____

2 16% of 26   = _____

3 72% of 105 = _____

4 11% of 5   = _____

5 52% of 91   = _____

6 33% of 99   = _____

7 89% of 246 = _____

8 20% of 10   = _____

Thursday

Tourist Trap!

Help Terra and Trekk calculate the prices for the souvenirs they want to buy. Multiply the price times the discount expressed as a decimal, then subtract the answer from the original price.

Example: 12% off toy beavers! Price was $4.75–you pay $4.18!
$0.12 \times \$4.75 = \$0.57$ discount
$\$4.75 - \$0.57 = \$4.18$

1. 25% off maple leaf jewelry! Was $22.50 – you pay $_____!

2. 33% off Hudson Bay picture frame! Was $21.75 – you pay $_____!

3. 5% off goose fridge magnets! Was $3.99 – you pay $_____!

4. 45% off maple chocolates! Was $10.49 – you pay $_____!

5. 17% off moose baseball caps! Was $11.65 – you pay $_____!

6. 22% off Canada puzzles! Was $8.50 – you pay $_____!

What A BIG Dog

Terra and Trekk were walking along the shore when a family came by with the biggest dog they ever saw! He was big, black, and the friendliest dog they had ever met. "What kind of dog is that?" they asked the family, as the dog licked their faces. "He's bigger than we are!"

"It's a Newfoundland dog! The best dog there is!" they said.

Terra couldn't wait to tell her friends about the Newfoundland dog. Help her write a postcard by adding adjectives to her letter:

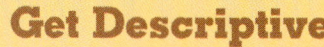

Get Descriptive

An *adjective* describes a noun or a pronoun.

amazing beautiful brave
clever cold deep
drowning enormous
exciting fabulous
fascinating helpless
little gigantic hard poor
powerful scary small stormy
strong surprised terrific wet

Now it's your turn! Write a story about how fun it would be to have a big old Newfoundland dog around the house! Don't forget to use lots of adjectives! Underline your adjectives.

Dear Tammy,

We saw a _____ dog called a Newfoundland dog! He looks like a _____ bear. He weighed 150 pounds and stood almost six feet tall! That's a _____ dog! He jumped on Trekk's shoulders and knocked him to the _____ ground! Newfoundland dogs are _____ swimmers, with webbed feet. They swim better than any other dog. They are very _____ and like to rescue _____ people in the water. They are _____ enough to pull _____ boats to shore, even in _____ weather. George Washington, Benjamin Franklin, and Lewis & Clark all had Newfoundland dogs. But he sure slobbered a lot. Trekk got all _____.

Terra

_____
_____
_____
_____
_____
_____
_____
_____
_____
_____
_____
_____
_____
_____
_____
_____
_____

Discover Seaman, the Newfoundland dog that traveled with Lewis & Clark on their voyage of discovery: http://www.id.blm.gov/lc/seaman.htm.

Friday

You've got a lot of living yet to do, but describe the happiest day of your life so far. What was involved? Who was involved? How did it change you?

_____

_____

_____

_____

_____

_____

_____

_____

_____

_____

_____

_____

_____

_____

_____

_____

"Their Fair Share of Fare!"

A little concerned over their food supply—but also for fun—Trekk and Terra decided to be extremely fair about dividing up the food. When they opened a can of peas, they counted the number of peas (there were 180) and divided them equally (each person got 60).

Terra pointed out that in terms of fractions each got 60/180 of the can. Trekk noted that 60/180 was really the same as 1/3–60/180 and 1/3 are therefore equivalent fractions—and it's a lot easier to work with 1/3!

Simplify the pairs of fractions below, then see if they are equivalent.

1. 6/12 and 4/8   Equivalent? _____

2. 5/15 and 4/20   Equivalent? _____

3. 12/40 and 9/30   Equivalent? _____

4. 27/30 and 45/50   Equivalent? _____

5. 28/77 and 20/44   Equivalent? _____

6. 36/44 and 24/38   Equivalent? _____

7. 17/19 and 153/171   Equivalent? _____

8. 45/55 and 36/44   Equivalent? _____

9. 12/63 and 40/96   Equivalent? _____

10. 27/72 and 80/96   Equivalent? _____

11. 144/288 and 216/432   Equivalent? _____

12. 63/81 and 77/99   Equivalent? _____

13. 117/143 and 98/112   Equivalent? _____

14. 212/324 and 42/72   Equivalent? _____

15. 333/999 and 222/666   Equivalent? _____

Busy Glaciers

12,000 years ago, almost all of Canada and much of the northern U.S. was buried by vast ice sheets called glaciers. These magnificent rivers of ice and snow carved much of the landscape in those areas, and although they have retreated, we still have some impressive glaciers left.

Glaciers form whenever more snow falls in the winter than melts in the summer. As the snow piles up, the older snow at the bottom compresses into ice. This part of the glacier is called the *accumulation zone*. Eventually, the weight of the ice causes it to flow downhill.

As glaciers flow, they scoop out great areas of rock and earth, which they push in front of themselves as big rubble piles called *moraines*. These moraines sometimes contain boulders as big as buildings.

Sometimes a glacier has another glacier, or *tributary glacier*, flowing into it. The area where a tributary glacier spills into a main glacier is called the *ogive*. The tributary glacier's moraine gets shoved into the bigger glacier in a dark line called a *lateral moraine*, which looks like a dark stripe going down the glacier. Eventually several of these lateral moraines join together into big thick stripes called *medial moraines,* making the glacier all striped.

Eventually the glacier reaches a point where it loses more ice through melting and the loss of ice blocks than it gains from the ice flow. That area of ice loss is called the *ablation zone* and it occurs at the end of a glacier. The surface of the glacier starts to break and gets covered with deep cracks called *crevasses*. The very end of a glacier, its *snout*, is where large blocks of ice fall off and the *meltwater* from the glacier flows out from underneath the glacier.

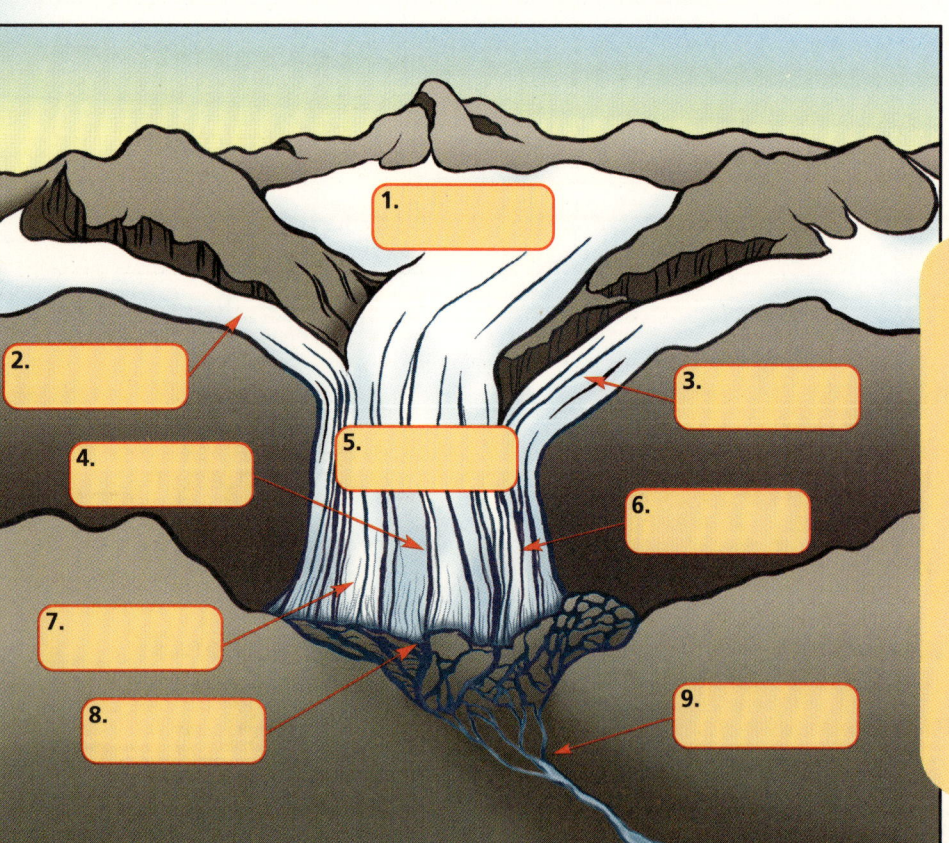

Use the reading above and the words below to name the parts of the glacier.

1.
2.
3.
4.
5.
6.
7.
8.
9.

Ablation zone

Lateral moraine

Snout

Tributary glacier

Crevasses

Meltwater

Medial moraine

Ogive

Accumulation zone

Swans in Flight

Migratory birds, such as the whistling swan, fly long distances. Scientists tag swans to help study their flights.

Below is a record of how many miles each of four swans flew over a week. Arrange the data in a bar graph. Use different colors for each bird. Study the data to determine the best amount to count by for the Y-axis. Fill in the numbers and label each axis.

	SWAN 1	SWAN 2	SWAN 3	SWAN 4
Mon.	74	37	18	42
Tue.	60	30	23	37
Wed.	44	22	34	8
Thu.	70	35	41	29
Fri.	40	20	37	15
Sat.	38	19	31	24
Sun.	52	26	24	32

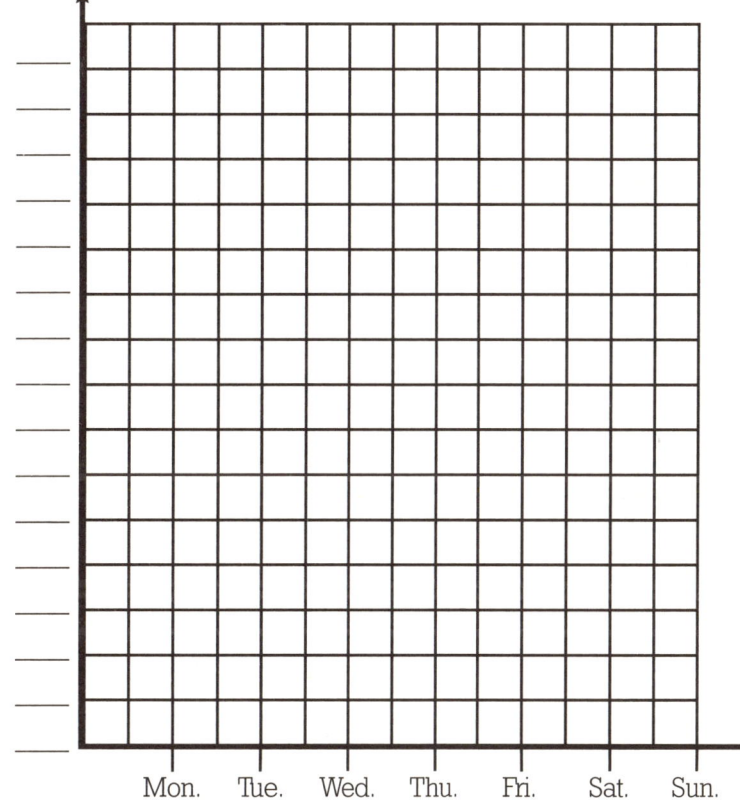

Y-axis: _____

Mon.   Tue.   Wed.   Thu.   Fri.   Sat.   Sun.

X-axis: _____

Determine the average amount of miles each swan flew per day. Add up the total number of miles for each swan and divide by the number of days.

Swan 1 _____   Swan 3 _____

Swan 2 _____   Swan 4 _____

More Mega Math

How many triangles add up to 8?

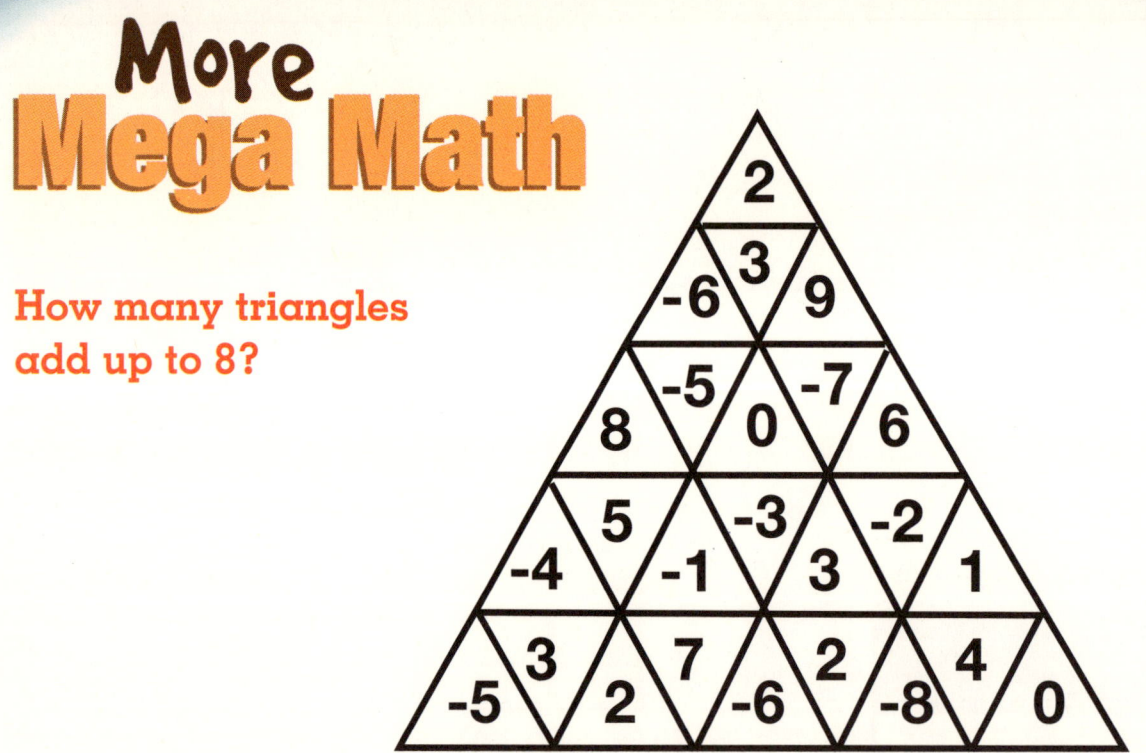

Brain Teaser

Which one doesn't belong?

cheese

rice

sponge

shoe

birthday

Fill in the Homonyms

Homonyms sound, or are spelled, the same but mean different things. Fill in the blanks below with the correct homonyms.

1 __I__ have an eyelash in my __eye__ .

2 My mother needs to go __~~by~~__ the bakery to __buy__ a cake.

3 Did you __~~do~~__ that, there are __~~there~~__ more tickets available?

4 My father's sister, __and__ Sara, has an __huge__ farm.

5 " __mom__ " did you find the Halloween costume you plan to __get__ ?

6 Sam's dad said, " __to__ , put on some sunblock. That _____ is really strong."

7 Did you _____ the teacher tell us to come over _____?

8 I _____ the book with the _____ cover.

9 I want _____ eat _____ cookies, _____.

10 Let's _____ at the market and buy the _____ for the cookout.

Hudson's Children

CHAPTER FIVE

Terra, Trekk and Trekk's dad stopped to show their passports at the border and headed northwest on Queen's Highway 17. They made camp for the night at Lake Superior Provincial Park. Both Trekk and Terra were excited to be in Canada. "Part of it," Trekk said, "just comes from small changes, like 'Queen's Highway 17' instead of a state road, and being in a 'Provincial Park' instead of a state park."

"I know," Terra said. "It just gives me a sense of a frontier because it's so different."

"Frontier," Trekk said. "It doesn't seem too wild to me. But it is different. Even the trash barrels in the park have MNR on them."

"In the States," his dad said, "we have departments of natural resources. Here, it's the Ministry of Natural Resources. These terms are left over from the days when Canada was part of Great Britain. Still, it was the French who were here first."

"Is that why signs are in both English and French?" Trekk asked.

"Exactly. Most people of Quebec, the next province east, speak French as their first language. They care deeply about their traditions. Some have even wanted independence from Canada."

"What about here in Ontario?" Trekk wondered.

"Ontario was originally part of Quebec, though the French had the first forts here, too. Immigrants from England and the United States settled the area. There were clashes between the groups, and Ontario split off. There is still a lot of French influence, especially as you go toward Quebec."

"How do you say 'moose' in French, Dad?" Trekk asked. "I want to see a moose."

"I don't know," his dad laughed. "I don't speak French. Maybe moose," he said in a terrible accent.

"That can't be right," Trekk said, as Terra made a face. Terra and Trekk woke early the next morning. They came out of their tents and decided to explore. In the early morning quiet, Trekk heard a rustling in the brush, just over a little rise beyond the campground.

"Terra, listen!" he said softly.

"I hear it," she responded. "Sshh," she hissed as Trekk started toward the sound. As quietly as they could, they moved closer to the crunching sound.

"Maybe it's our moose," Terra whispered.

"Or a bear," Trekk said. The noise grew louder as they crawled closer. Lying flat, skin crawling, they peered cautiously over the edge of the rise. A crash of brush made Terra and Trekk jump. In a flurry of twigs and dry leaves, a grey squirrel bounded away.

Terra laughed. "Some wilderness," Trekk said disgustedly.

Monday

Activity 5

Skill: Summarizing

Write the name of the place that matches each of the following descriptions. Not all words will be used.

Chicago   Mackinaw City

Ann Arbor   Escanaba

Detroit   Whitefish Point

White Cloud   Sault Ste. Marie

Milwaukee   Lake Superior Provincial Park

Petoskey   Thunder Bay

1. Terra joins Trekk and her Uncle Phil. _____

2. Terra breathes in "the world at its best." _____

3. Trekk takes an unexpected swim. _____

4. "Mighty Mac" spans the Straits. _____

5. The travelers visit the Great Lakes Shipwreck Museum. _____

6. The travelers cross the border. _____

7. Trekk and Terra face a "wild animal." _____

Math Maze

Where Do You Finish?

- Begin with "16" in the upper left-hand corner.

- Moving down or horizontally to the left or right, choose the correct path to arrive at a three-digit number whose digits are all the same.

- NOTE: You must stay on the gridlines as you move and do not backtrack.

- Each "square" is worth -8. All circled numbers are to be added.

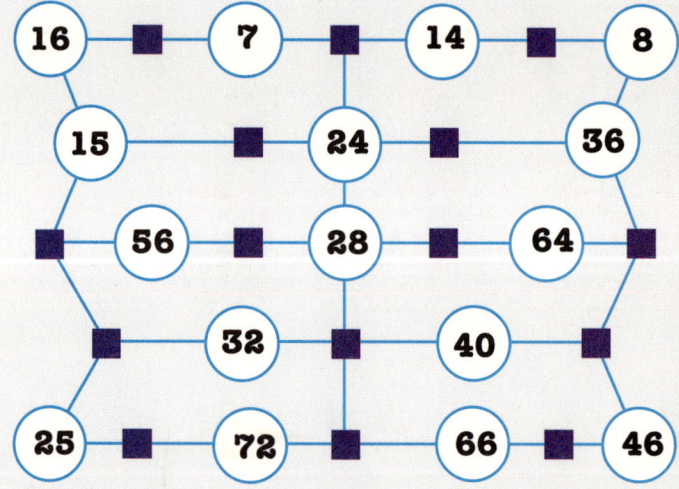

For example:
25 ■ 10 = 27   (25 - 8 = 17 + 10 = 27)

Word Games

Can you guess the relationship?

1 cork   ice   boat   wood

2 scorpion   wasp   jellyfish   nettles

3 John   Abraham   George   Ronald

62

NO BONES ABOUT IT

Match the bones to the part of the body. If you need help,
use an encyclopedia or the Internet.

1. humerus

a. knee

2. femur

b. shoulder

3. ulna

c. upper arm

4. fibula

d. chest

5. sternum

e. neck

6. patella

f. lower leg

7. scapula

g. forearm

8. cervical vertebrae

h. thigh

GET BACK ON TRACK!

Terra once read that pioneers made "corduroy roads" from logs. One day, when their truck got stuck on a mud road, Trekk found five piles of boards, each with different-sized boards. Based on the size of their truck, Terra figured they'd need at least 115 square meters of board to get back to the road.

Help Trekk and Terra calculate the area of the boards in each pile of boards. Will they need all 5 piles to get back to the road? How many square meters will they have left over? They've already done the first one for you!

Pile #1: Nine 1 meter x 4 meter boards

Each board is 1 m x 4 m = 4 square meters

9 x 4 square meters = 36 square meters

Pile #2: Six 3 meter x 2.5 meter boards

_____

_____

Pile #3: Two 1.5 meter x 6 meter boards

_____

_____

Pile #4: Six 0.5 meter x 8 meter boards

_____

_____

_____

Pile #5: Three 2.0 meter x 2.5 meter boards

_____

_____

Pile #1 = 36 square meters
+
Pile #2 = ____ square meters
+
Pile #3 = ____ square meters
+
Pile #4 = ____ square meters
+
Pile #5 = ____ square meters

Total   = ____ square meters
-            115 square meters
m² left over = ____

Mega Math

Use pennies, nickels, dimes, quarters, half dollars, and silver dollars to solve these problems.

Holly is saving money for a new soccer ball. She has saved $55.02 so far. If she has an equal number of four different coins, which coins does she have? How many of each?

Comparative and Superlative

**Some adjectives, usually those with two or more syllables, use "more" and "most" to form their comparative and superlative forms.
Fill in the blanks below.**

	Word	Comparative	Superlative
1	horrible	_____	_____
2	generous	_____	_____
3	terrific	_____	_____
4	delicious	_____	_____
5	ridiculous	_____	_____
6	complicated	_____	_____

Thursday

Pie Graphs

Total Cities A-F Population = 500,500

To find the population for each individual city, change the percent to a decimal and multiply by the total population of 500,500. The first one is done for you.

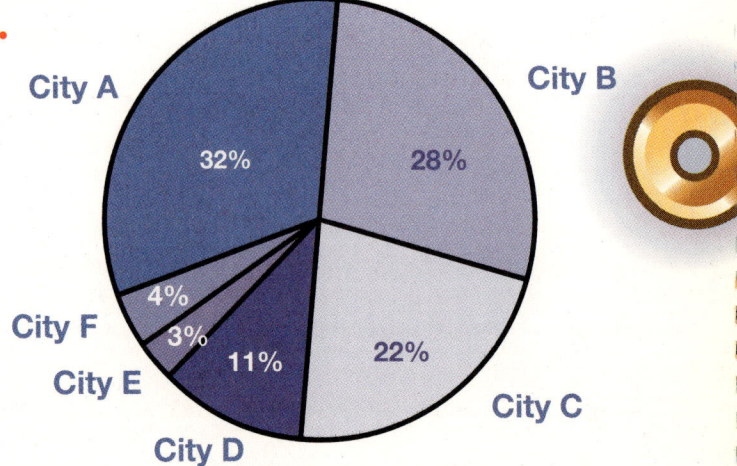

City A 32%
City B 28%
City C 22%
City D 11%
City E 3%
City F 4%

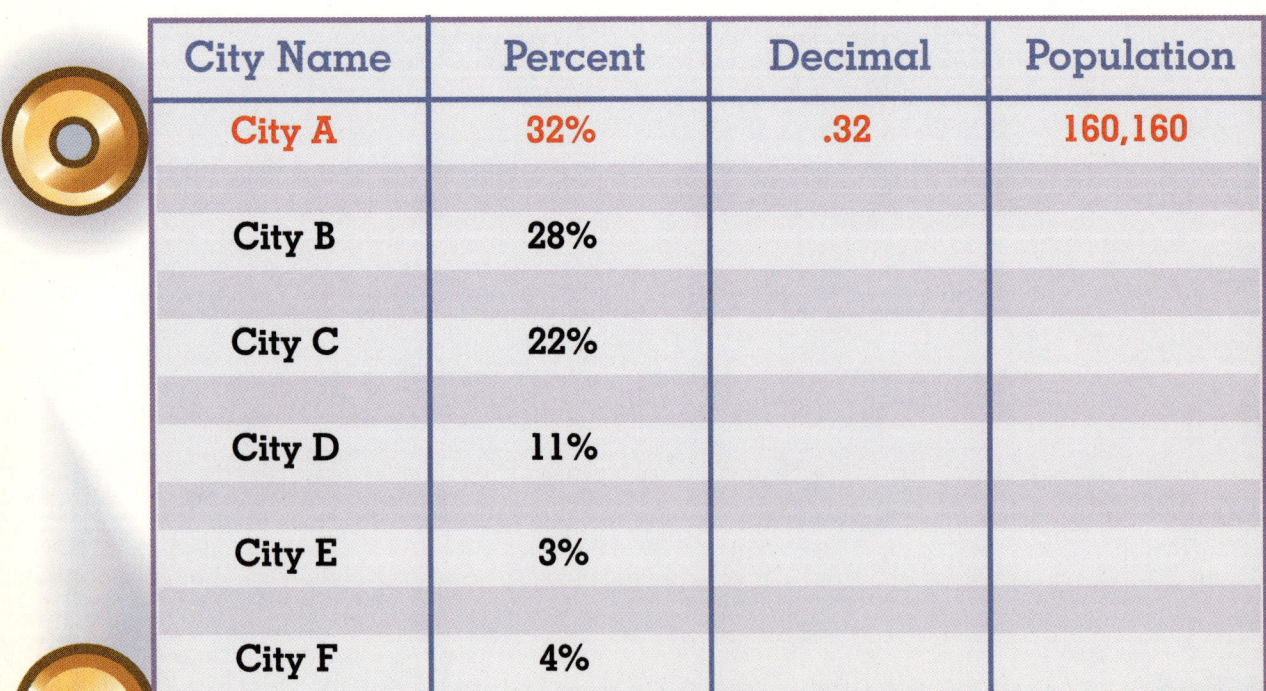

City Name	Percent	Decimal	Population
City A	32%	.32	160,160
City B	28%		
City C	22%		
City D	11%		
City E	3%		
City F	4%		

Mad Inventors!

"Do you know who invented the television?" Dad asked.

"I don't know, but he was a genius," said Trekk.

"Reginald Fessenden, a Canadian inventor, patented a TV. But really, the TV evolved from smaller inventions." Dad looked at Trekk in the rearview mirror. "So do sentences with appositives. Appositives are phrases that help explain a noun or pronoun. They can be long or short and can come at the beginning, middle or end of a sentence. Let's invent some sentences with appositives. Here's one: Gideon Sundback invented the zipper, a new way to fasten clothes."

"I get it," Terra chimed in. "Alexander Graham Bell, the inventor of the telephone, was born in Scotland in 1847."

Combine the following sentences into one sentence by making one of the sentences an appositive.

1. Louis-Jacques-Mandé Daguerre was born near Paris, France. He developed the first photograph in 1826-1827.

   Louis-Jacques-Mandé Daguerre, the developer of the first photograph in 1826-1827, was born near Paris, France.

2. In 1924, John Larson created the polygraph test. A polygraph test is also known as a lie detector test.

   _____

   _____

3. DVDs were invented in 1995. DVDs have better quality pictures than videocassettes.

   _____

   _____

4. The game of basketball was created by James Naismith. James Naismith was a physical education teacher.

   _____

   _____

5. Cell phones were invented in 1988. Cell phones allow people to call friends from anywhere.

   _____

   _____

Friday

A brief description of an idea for a movie, including its storyline and characters, is called a "treatment." Write a "treatment" starring yourself in a new movie. It can be an action/thriller, a drama, a horror film, or a comedy.

_____

_____

_____

_____

_____

_____

_____

_____

_____

_____

_____

_____

_____

_____

_____

"Percentage Advantage!"

Trekk, Terra, and Dad drove over the Mackinac Bridge, which was 5 miles long, but it was 100 miles total to their next campsite. This means they were only able to move 5/100 of the way, or 5%.

A percentage shows a fraction of a whole. 100% would be the same as a whole, while 50% would be half, and 25% would be a quarter.

You can also think of a penny as being 1% of a dollar, while 5 pennies is 5%, and 100 pennies would be 100% (or the WHOLE dollar!).

Try and determine the percentage for each amount.

1. What percentage of the pizza has been eaten?

2. The boy started with a dollar and fifty cents, but then bought 3 candy bars that cost 10 cents each. What percentage of his money has he spent?

3. The tree branch is two feet long (or 24 inches). The worm has crawled 6 inches. What percentage of the branch has he covered?

4. A waffle has 100 squares. If you've eaten 90 squares, what percentage of the waffle is left?

5. Trekk shared a candy bar with Terra. She ate 5 squares. Trekk ate the remaining 10 squares. What percentage did Trekk eat?

6. Terra is making a paper flower. What percentage of the petals will be blue?

The Long Way Home

When cold weather comes to Canada, many birds migrate south in search of food and warmer weather.

At right is a calendar with the number of swans sighted each day during their migration. Calculate the average and **mode** for each week.

October

Sun.	Mon.	Tue.	Wed.	Thu.	Fri.	Sat.
	1 0	2 200	3 250	4 250	5 600	6 1200
7 1200	8 1200	9 1300	10 2000	11 4000	12 6000	13 9000
14 10,000	15 10,000	16 13,000	17 13,000	18 15,000	19 13,000	20 12,000
21 11,000	22 11,000	23 10,000	24 10,000	25 10,000	26 10,000	27 8,000
28 7,000	29 400	30 400	31 100			

Mode is the number in a set that occurs most often. The mode for Week 1 is 250. The mode can help you make predictions. For example, if you walk into a store and most of the candy bars cost $1, you can be pretty certain that any candy bar you buy will be $1.

When you're through, plot the mean and mode for each week in a line graph using two different colors. Remember to label each axis. Choose the best number to count by for your Y-axis based on the data.

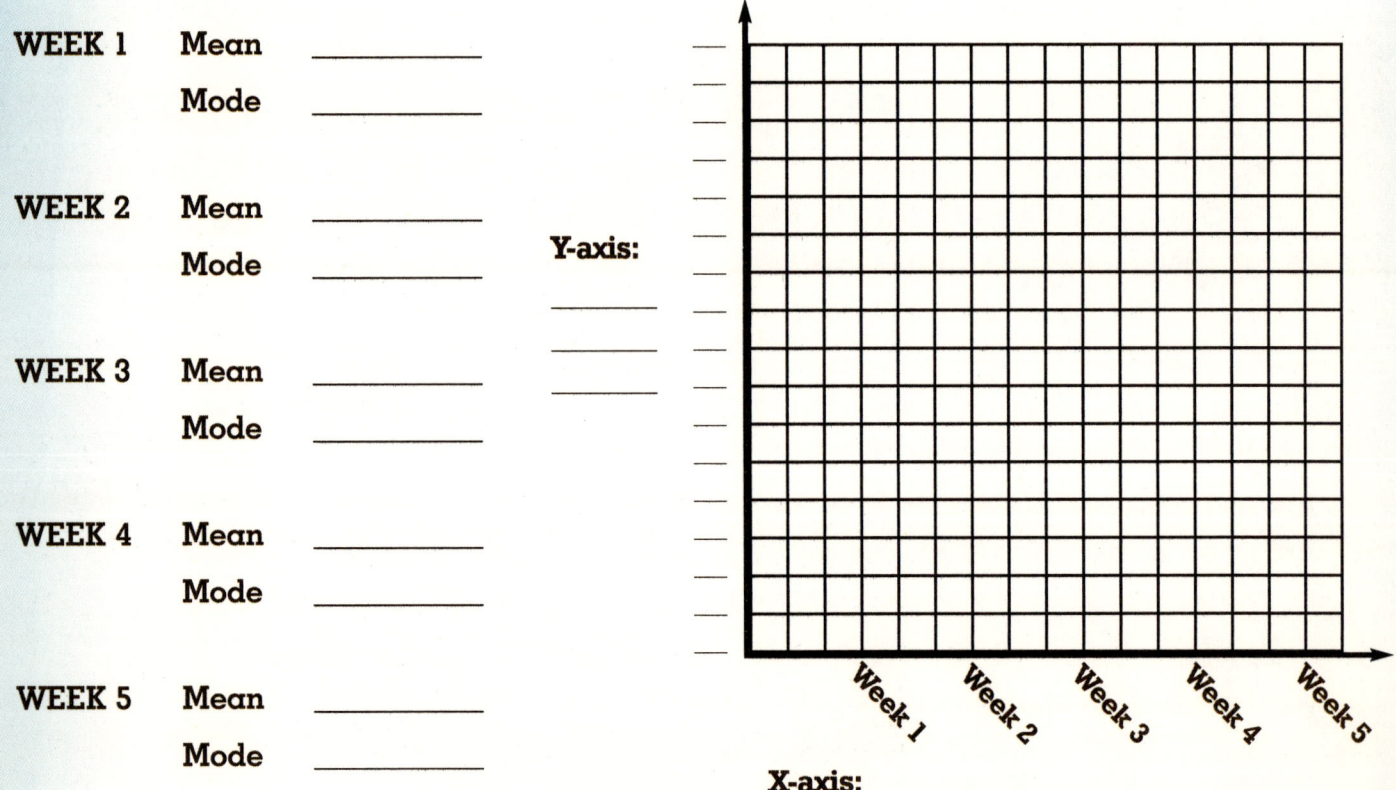

WEEK 1   Mean   _____
           Mode   _____

WEEK 2   Mean   _____
           Mode   _____

WEEK 3   Mean   _____
           Mode   _____

WEEK 4   Mean   _____
           Mode   _____

WEEK 5   Mean   _____
           Mode   _____

Y-axis: _____

X-axis: _____

How does the mode differ from the average?

_____

It's for the Birds!

Canadian geese, cranes, and whistling swans are among the migratory birds captured, then tagged, at a bird refuge near Ontario. Some of the birds are already found to have tags, however, either from Canadian or U.S. bird sanctuaries.

Fill in the missing information in the chart below.

Canadian Geese		
Number captured	20	100%
Number with U.S. tag	5	25%
Number with Canadian tag	7	35%
Number untagged	8	40%

Cranes		
Number captured	16	
Number with U.S. tag		25%
Number with Canadian tag	8	
Number untagged	4	

Atlantic Brants		
Number captured		100%
Number with U.S. tag	5	
Number with Canadian tag	5	
Number untagged	10	

Harlequin Ducks		
Number captured	50	
Number with U.S. tag	10	
Number with Canadian tag	24	
Number untagged		32%

Whistling Swans		
Number captured		100%
Number with U.S. tag		15%
Number with Canadian tag		35%
Number untagged	20	

Snow Geese		
Number captured		
Number with U.S. tag	34	
Number with Canadian tag	88	
Number untagged	78	

Common Eiders		
Number captured		100%
Number with U.S. tag	27	
Number with Canadian tag	15	
Number untagged	18	

Black Ducks		
Number captured	90	
Number with U.S. tag		40%
Number with Canadian tag	27	
Number untagged		

Common Terns		
Number captured	500	
Number with U.S. tag		24%
Number with Canadian tag		
Number untagged		51%

More Mega Math

Each of the symbols below represents a number between 1 - 10. Can you figure out which number should fill in the blank?

Converting Fractions to Decimals

1 $\dfrac{17}{1000}$ = _____

2 $5\dfrac{199}{1000}$ = _____

3 $6\dfrac{35}{10000}$ = _____

4 $\dfrac{999}{10000}$ = _____

5 $5\dfrac{5}{1000}$ = _____

6 $792\dfrac{1777}{10000}$ = _____

7 $\dfrac{84}{1000}$ = _____

8 $2\dfrac{27}{10000}$ = _____

Fantasy vs. Reality

Realistic writing is based on events that could happen.
Fantasy writing is based on events that could never happen.

Circle Fantasy or Reality for each sentence below.

1 The dog was bigger than a skyscraper.   Fantasy   Reality

2 Our football team won every game this season.   Fantasy   Reality

3 Mary's cat asked her, "When will dinner be ready?"   Fantasy   Reality

4 Sam, my brother, can fly higher than an eagle.   Fantasy   Reality

5 The doctor cured the patient.   Fantasy   Reality

6 The creepy, old house called to me.   Fantasy   Reality

7 My father is an award-winning writer.   Fantasy   Reality

8 The slimy monster slithered out of the creek and   Fantasy   Reality
sang songs.

Hudson's Children

CHAPTER SIX

The three went for a swim in Lake Superior before leaving the park. None were prepared for how cold the water was. They ate lunch on the beach and felt a little foolish as they huddled in jackets while people walked past in bathing suits.

Driving northwest, they pulled off the highway briefly to see one of the most photographed sites in Ontario, the famous goose statue in Wawa. The two-ton goose had a twenty-foot wingspan. "Why did they put this here, Dad?" Trekk asked.

"When the Trans-Canadian highway went through, local businesspeople wanted something to get people to stop here."

"Why a goose?" Terra wondered.

"Well, 'Wawa' means 'Land of the Big Goose' or 'Wild Goose' in Ojibway. You know, I was wrong when I said that the French were the first to settle in Canada. Native peoples settled here centuries before Europeans came. A lot of place names around here are Ojibway, as are some that you already know, such as 'Mississippi' and 'Milwaukee.'"

"You don't know French, but you know Ojibway?" Terra asked. Her uncle grinned.

"This one I studied. The Ojibway were once one of the largest groups in North America. Some people think they migrated here from the Hudson Bay area."

"Oh," Trekk said. "I had forgotten about the Hudson part of this trip."

"Well, I hadn't," his dad said. "Though I haven't had a great idea yet."

"Don't worry," Terra said. "You will."

"Or we will," Trekk added.

As they drove on through the day, Trekk and Terra noted that there were fewer and fewer signs of human activity. "Not much out here," Trekk said.

"What are those, Uncle Phil?" Terra asked. At the side of the highway was a small road leading into the woods. Behind the trees, she could see an opening. She had seen several of these on the way.

"Those are what's left of construction camps. When they built the road, they'd clear a space to park the equipment as they went along. Let's pull in and have a look."

The truck followed the narrow entry into a sandy clearing. They drove to the edge and then circled back toward the highway. The truck's wheels began to spin. The truck slowed and then stopped.

Getting out of the truck, they noticed the wheels sinking in the sandy soil. "It's too soft," Trekk's dad said. He tried rocking the truck gently, then harder. The truck's wheels just sank deeper. The rear axles were down in the sand, and the nose pointed skyward like a sinking ship. Daylight was fading.

"Looks like we're spending the night here," Trekk's dad said. Trekk and Terra looked to the edge of the clearing. Not a sound could be heard from the road or the darkening woods.

Monday

Activity 6

Skill: Reading Comprehension

1. Why did Terra and Trekk feel foolish as they ate lunch on the beach?

   _____

   _____

2. Who are the Ojibway?

   _____

   _____

3. What does the Ojibway word "*Wawa*" mean?

   _____

   _____

4. Why was the statue of the goose built?

   _____

5. What did Trekk and Terra notice about the countryside as they traveled through the day?

   _____

6. Why were the clearings built alongside the highway?

   _____

7. Why couldn't Terra, Trekk and his dad return to the highway?

   _____

8. How will being stuck affect the trip?

   _____

Odd Number Out

Can you figure out which number doesn't belong?
Circle the correct answer.

1   29   7   35   11   43

2   17   19   37   18   47

3   53   7   67   13   88

Comparative and Superlative Exceptions

Some adjectives form the comparative and superlative by making a complete change in their form. Fill in the blanks below.

	Word	Comparative	Superlative
1	good	better	best
2	less	_____	_____
3	some	_____	_____
4	bad	_____	_____

WHO SAID IT?

Match the quotes to the people who said them. If you need help, use an encyclopedia or the Internet.

1. "I have a dream..."

a. Yogi Berra

2. "Give me liberty or give me death."

b. Benjamin Franklin

3. "That's one small step for man, one giant leap for mankind."

c. Albert Einstein

4. "Three may keep a secret, if two are dead."

d. Abraham Lincoln

5. "It ain't over 'til it's over."

e. Dr. Martin Luther King, Jr.

6. "Those who deny freedom to others, deserve it not for themselves; and, under a just God, can not long retain it."

f. John F. Kennedy

7. "Ask not what your country can do for you, but what you can do for your country."

g. Patrick Henry

8. "I think and think for months and years. Ninety-nine times the conclusion is false. The hundredth time I am right."

h. Neil Armstrong

SAIL AWAY!

After Mr. Guindon pulled Trekk from the lake, he asked Trekk to help him change the torn sail on his boat, the Sunfish. Mr. Guindon didn't have a spare sail that would fit, so he and Trekk went shopping for a new one. If the Sunfish is going to get just the right amount of wind power, it needs a triangle sail that is 18 square feet (or 1.7 square meters). Calculate the area of each triangle to find out which sail they should buy.

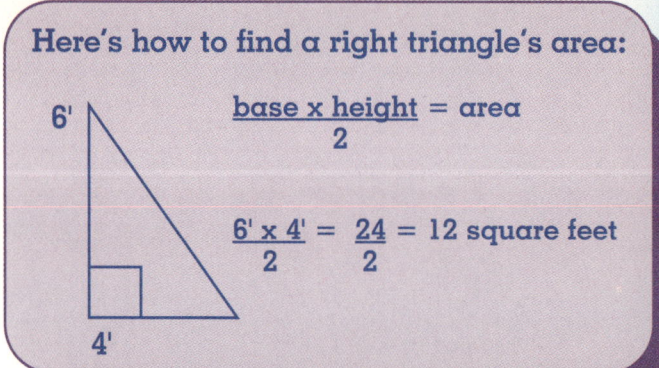

Here's how to find a right triangle's area:

$$\frac{base \times height}{2} = area$$

$$\frac{6' \times 4'}{2} = \frac{24}{2} = 12 \text{ square feet}$$

1. Base – 4' (1.2 m)

   Height – 8' (2.5 m)

   Area: _____

Wave Crasher

4. Base – 4' (1.2 m)

   Height – 10' (3 m)

   Area: _____

Surf Hopper

2. Base – 5' (1.5 m)

   Height – 7' (2.1 m)

   Area: _____

Foam Jumper

5. Base – 3' (1 m)

   Height – 11' (3.3 m)

   Area: _____

Shark Tail

3. Base – 4' (1.2 m)

   Height – 9' (2.8 m)

   Area: _____

Blue Thunder

6. Base – 5' (1.5 m)

   Height – 9' (2.8 m)

   Area: _____

Wind Shear

Mega Math

Can you solve the following problem? Assign different values for consonants and vowels. Can you detect a rule for solving the unknown amount?

Fall was approaching. Martine and Kevin went to buy school supplies. Together they bought:

- Backpack $22.00

- Markers $19.00

- Paints   ?

How much did the paints cost? What's the rule?

Riddles

1 I am found in the sea and on land but I do not walk or swim. I travel by foot but I am toeless. No matter where I go, I'm never far from home. What am I?

_____

2 I don't have lungs or a chest but I need air; I am not alive, but I grow; I don't have a mouth and I don't like water. What am I?

_____

3 My name means something that's used in an instrument that determines how hot you are. I'm also the name of a planet. Who am I?

_____

Thursday

Optical Illusions

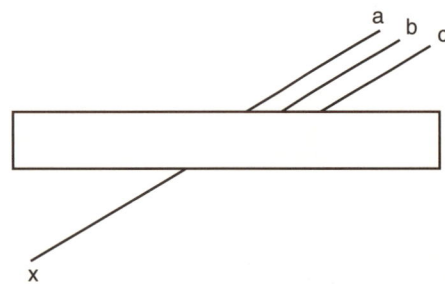

Which line is connected to line x? Line a, b or c?

Does there appear to be gray circles at the intersections of the white lines? Focus on any of the circles and they disappear!

Is the small box sitting in the corner of a wall or is it attached to a larger box?

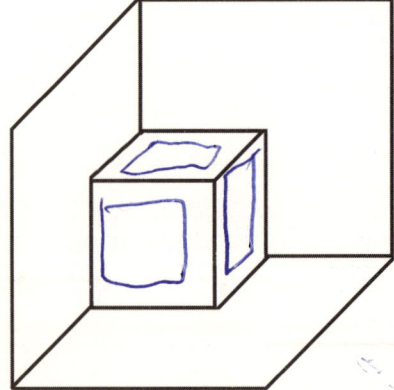

Vital Verbs

Terra and Trekk visited a museum with an exhibit on settlers' lives. Fascinated by the settlers, they decided to summarize the pioneer's letter below for their friends. Help Terra and Trekk rewrite the antique letter into a story about the settlers, converting present and future tense verbs to past tense, and converting the first person (I, we) to third person (he, she, they).

I am so very excited, Peter. We got word from the Canadian government that we are receiving free land in the prairies. There has been no time for anything but packing and preparing for the trip. We are waiting at the last trading post, gathering the rest of our supplies. We do not have the money to buy a wagon, so we will be going west on an ox cart that my father is building. He is making the cart completely out of wood. Instead of using iron to hold the frames, he is using wooden pegs. You might think waiting is tiresome, but I am always out exploring. I watch the traders trade for furs and game meat. I watch laborers build the railway, which will go from the Atlantic to the Pacific! The journey to the prairies will be difficult, but it's fun to see so many new things.

Now rewrite the letter. The introduction has been done for you.
He received word from his family that he would be moving to western Canada. The Canadian government offered free land to people who moved to the prairies. _____

_____

_____

_____

_____

_____

_____

_____

_____

Friday

Newsflash! You've been given the lead story assignment for your neighborhood's newspaper "Talk of the Town." Write a one-page feature article on something or someone interesting that is a part of your neighborhood.

_____

_____

_____

_____

_____

_____

_____

_____

_____

_____

_____

_____

_____

_____

_____

_____

_____

Ratio Riddles!

1. Welcome to the weekend! You get to play every Saturday and Sunday! If that's true, what's the proportion of weekend days to all days in a year, assuming one year has 52 weeks? If you go to school for six more years, what's the proportion of weekend days to all days over six years?

2. You go to scary movies on the weekend! Look around the theater. There are 36 people in the theater, so there are 72 hands in the room covering the eyes of all those faces. What is the proportion of fingers (not thumbs) to hands in the room? What's the proportion of fingers to eyes in the room?

3. *Splat!* The guy in the grocery store knocks over all the egg cartons. One egg in each carton of six eggs breaks. Yuck! What's the proportion of broken eggs in each carton?

4. Every day you eat breakfast, lunch, and dinner. If you do this for six months running, what's the proportion of lunches to all your meals? How does that compare to the ratio of dinners to all your meals?

5. Every seven minutes you watch TV, you have to endure one minute and 30 seconds of commercials. Who needs this? If you watch TV for 12 hours on the weekend, what is the proportion of time you spend watching commercials to the time you spend watching TV shows?

6. *Where's the beef?* You ate 125 burgers last year, but only 3/8 of each burger was actually meat. The rest was bun. Lots of bun. Bun, bun, bun. What's the proportion of bun to meat that you ate last year in all those burgers?

7. *Say what?* If you spend forty seconds out of every three minutes talking, what proportion of a 16-hour day do you spend talking in relation to silent time?

8. Final riddle. Name one secret that you've discovered about ratios. Hint: What do ratios really tell you? C'mon!

Current Events!

Did you know that the ocean is largely responsible for the world's temperatures?

Ocean water at the equator warms up and ocean currents drive that water north or south. These currents warm the air around them. As the water nears the poles, though, the water gets cold. The ocean currents then drive that cold water back toward the equator, where the water warms up again.

Many things affect how ocean currents work, including the amount of salt in solution in the water. If too much of the world's ice melts and adds more fresh water to the ocean, then the decreased amount of salt in solution might turn some of the ocean currents off. If that happened, all the warm temperatures brought to Europe by the Gulf Stream ocean current would go away and Europe would become mighty cold!

Below is a map of the world's ocean currents. Based on your knowledge of geography, try to write the name of each of the ocean's currents from the list. Then, knowing that warm water moves toward the poles and cold water moves toward the equator, use blue and red markers to indicate which currents have warm water and which have cold water.

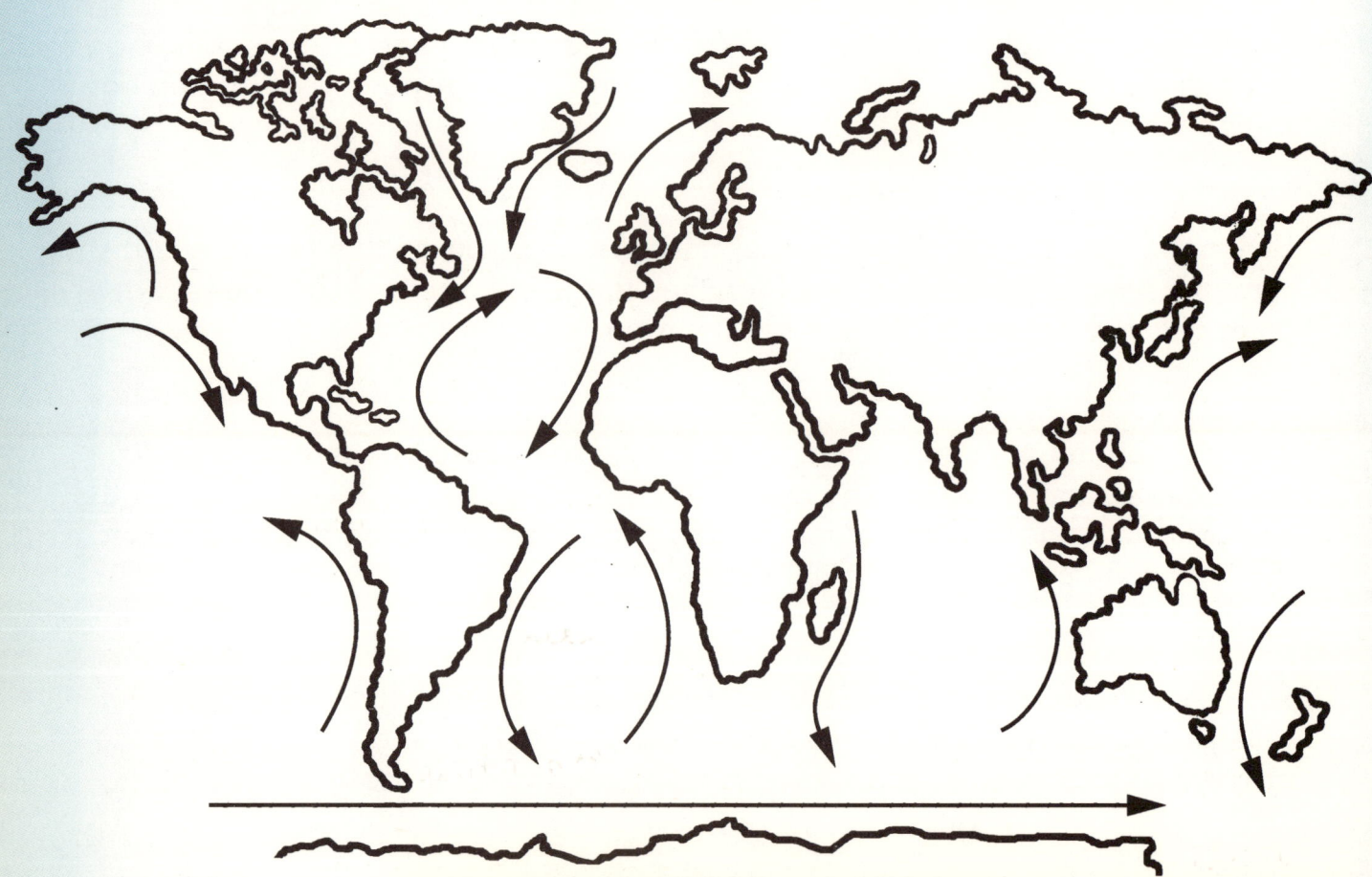

Ocean Currents

Alaska	Benguela	East Greenland	Labrador
Canary	Brazil	East Australia	Oyashio
Gulf Stream	Mozambique	Peru	Antarctic Circumpolar
Norwegian	West Australia	California	Kuroshio

What's the Solution?

You've learned that salt dissolved in ocean water helps to determine world temperatures. But many other substances can dissolve in water: sugar, baking soda, and even carbon dioxide.

Did you know, however, that you can only dissolve so much salt or sugar in water? The maximum amount of a substance you can dissolve is called that substance's *solubility*. When you hit that maximum, you have *saturated* the solution. The higher the temperature of the liquid, the higher the *saturation point*.

The saturation point is always expressed as a *ratio*. If the saturation point for sugar in water is 1:10, that is, 1 part of sugar for 10 parts of a liquid, then you'll need 3 parts of sugar to saturate 30 parts of water (3:30).

Find the missing numbers in the saturation point experiments below:

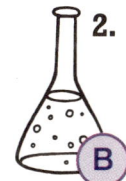

1. Ratio for saturation – 1:10
                Water – 500 parts
                Sugar – _____ parts

A

Sugar and Water

4. Ratio for saturation – 10:17
                Water – 595 parts
     Carbon Dioxide – _____ parts

D

Carbon Dioxide and Water (soda)

2. Ratio for saturation – 7:20
                Water – _____ parts
                 Salt – 49 parts

B

Salt and Water

5. Ratio for saturation – 7:26
                Water – _____ parts
      Baking Soda – 147 parts

E

Baking Soda and Water

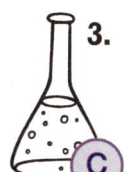

3. Ratio for saturation – _____
                Water – 150 parts
         Fertilizer – 60 parts

C

Fertilizer (potassium nitrate) and Water

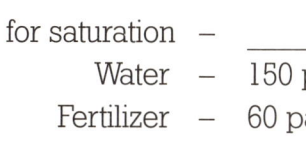

6. Ratio for saturation – 5:21
                Water – 525 parts
                 Lye – _____ parts

F

Lye and Water

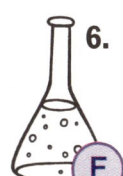

More Mega Math

How many squares add up to 5?

0	-3	5	-4	1	-5
6	2	1	0	-2	8
2	-3	4	3	7	-9
-1	0	-2	0	1	10
1	5	-8	9	-6	0
2	2	6	-2	7	4

Word Pictures

Can you guess what these mean?

1. **PERSONALITY** *split personality*

2. **splostace** *lost in space*

3. **READ** *Read between the Lines*

4. **BOTTIMETLE** *Time in a bottle*

5. **STRAWBERRY CAKE** *strawberry short cake*

6. **TOMORROW DAY** *Day after tomorrow*

7. **LIVE LEARN** *Live and Learn*

8. **TUNNEL●** *Light at the end of the tunnel*

Optical Illusions

Can you guess what these mean?

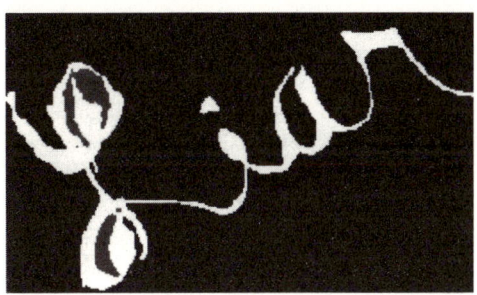

Do you see the word "Liar"?
What else do you see?

Do you see circles at the
line intersections? In reality,
there are none!

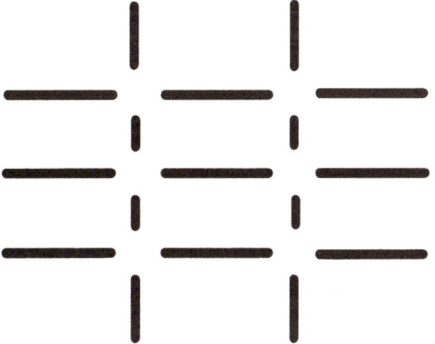

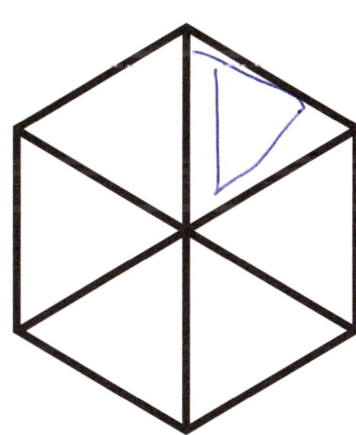

Is the card folded
toward you or away
from you?

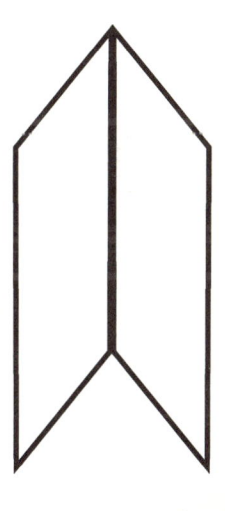

There are two objects in this
figure. One is a hexagon.
What is the other? Triangle

Hudson's Children

CHAPTER SEVEN

Trekk and Terra felt a little nervous that night as they set up camp. Being alone out here was different from being in an area set aside for camping.

"So, do you want to see a bear tonight, Trekk?" Terra grinned.

Trekk grinned back. "This is a good night for it. Wolves, too." That night, after letting the fire go out, Trekk and Tara stared up into the night sky. The number of stars they could see always amazed the cousins when they were far enough away from the city to see all of them. Yet, they were aware that things were different, and neither Trekk nor Terra slept well. Both woke several times in the night and listened hard.

The next morning, Trekk's dad continued trying to get the truck loose. He tried gently rocking again, first shifting into reverse, and then going forward to gain momentum. By now the truck had dug itself so far down that he made little progress. Trekk and Tara collected brush and wedged it under the tires to try to get some traction. This time the truck moved a little, but then it spewed out the branches and sank back.

Terra remembered reading about pioneer "corduroy roads" made out of logs. She and Trekk found some dead trees and used an axe to cut them. Trekk's dad dug out some more sand, trying to make the slope less steep. They carefully placed the logs near the rear wheels. Gently, Trekk's dad eased the truck onto the logs and out of the hole the tires had dug. They all cheered as the truck rose, but they soon fell into silence. No matter how gently Trekk's dad tried to drive, the truck just began sinking again.

"We might have to build this corduroy road back to the highway," Terra said. "Or at least back to where the sand was firmer."

"That could take days," Trekk wailed.

"We could do what we just did, and gain a few feet at a time," his dad said. "That would save cutting trees to build a whole road." His dad sent Trekk to the highway to watch for passing cars. Trekk waited and waited, looking up and down the empty road, but no one came. As the afternoon shadows lengthened, it became clear that they would be out here for another night. Trekk rejoined his father and cousin.

"I want to get out of here," Trekk complained.

"You wanted adventure," Terra pointed out.

"Don't remind me," Trekk said, looking down as evening closed in.

Monday

Activity 7

Skill: Predicting

Write a prediction in response to each of the following questions. Be sure to write complete sentences.

1. What would you do if you were in the same situation as Terra, Trekk and Trekk's dad?

   _____
   _____
   _____

2. Do you think the travelers will see bear, moose or wolves before they get out? Why?

   _____
   _____

3. If you had a similar adventure, would you feel nervous about spending the night in the wilderness? Why?

   _____
   _____

4. Would you have come back to the clearing, as Trekk did? Why?

   _____
   _____

5. What other problems or dangers do the travelers face as they try to free the truck?

   _____
   _____

6. How do you think they will get out of the clearing?

   _____
   _____

Math Maze

Break it in half!

- The object is to reduce your number until you arrive at a total of "16."

- Begin at the number "40" in the top left corner and choose the correct path to the bottom.

- Each time you cross a "triangle" you must divide your number by two, then proceed to add the next circled number to your total.

- You may go across or down but remember to stay on the lines.

- Also, remember that the "triangle" means that you divide your number by two (or break it in half!).

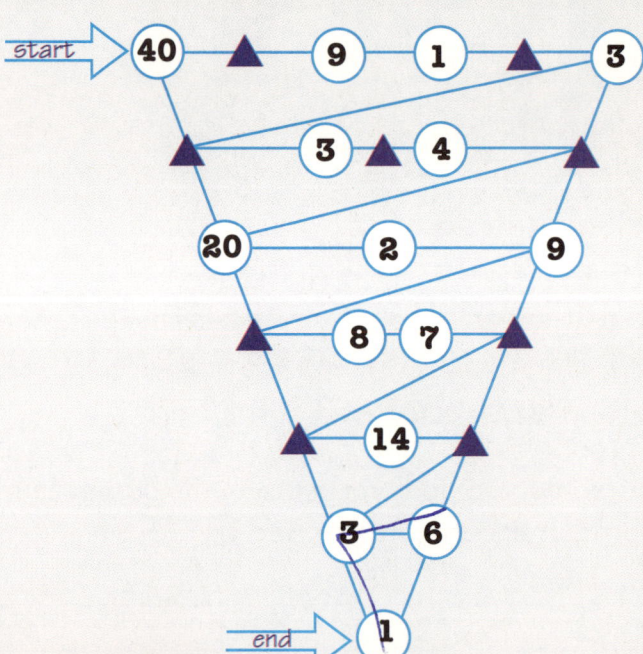

For example:

20 ▲ 7 = 17 (20 ÷ 2 = 10 + 7 = 17)

No Double Negatives

Never use double negatives when you write or speak. Correct the sentences below to eliminate the double negative.

1 She didn't say nothing.

_____

2 There weren't no shoes left in my size.

_____

3 He doesn't know nobody in his new school.

_____

4 Don't leave none of the milk in your glass.

_____

HELP WANTED

Match the professional titles to their area of expertise.
If you need help, use an encyclopedia or the Internet.

1. optometrist

a. language

2. botanist

b. fossils

3. entomologist

c. skin

4. geologist

d. insects

5. podiatrist

e. eyes

6. dermatologist

f. feet

7. paleontologist

g. earth

8. etymologist

h. plants

Finding Radius, Diameter and Circumference

Circumference measures the distance around a circle. To find circumference of a circle, multiply the diameter by three. To find diameter, multiply the radius by two. To find the radius, divide diameter by two. Fill in the missing data below. The first one is done for you.

Circumference   Diameter   Radius

	Circumference	Diameter	Radius
1.	6 feet	2 feet	1 foot
2.		14 cm	
3.	36 meters		
4.			4 mm
5.			812 cm
6.		25 miles	
7.	933 inches		
8.			51.2 yards
9.		.88 km	
10.	1,263 feet		
11.		7,612 cm	
12.			.115 mm
13.	573 meters		
14.		.999 cm	

Mega Math

Use pennies, nickels, dimes, quarters, half dollars, and silver dollars to solve these problems.

To raise money for new uniforms the football team is selling candy. After one week they have made $22.92. There is an equal number of coins. What coins do they have? How many of each?

Ratio Quiz

Match each statement to the correct set of numbers.

1 Two numbers that add to 36 and are in a 1:2 ratio

a 40, 10

2 Two numbers that add to 130 and are in a 6:7 ratio

b 50, 20

3 Two numbers that add to 50 and are in a 4:1 ratio

c 12, 24

4 Two numbers that add to 48 and are in a 1:1 ratio

d 50, 120

5 Two numbers that add to 70 and are in a 5:2 ratio

e 24, 24

6 Two numbers that add to 170 and are in a 5:12 ratio

f 60, 70

Thursday

Place Value with Decimals

Record each number on the place value chart.
The first one is done for you.

	Hundreds	Tens	Ones	And	Tenths	Hundredths	Thousandths
1.	6	4	9	•	6	9	2
2.				•			
3.				•			
4.				•			
5.				•			
6.				•			

1 six hundred forty-nine and six hundred ninety-two thousandths

2 fifty-one and five thousandths

3 seven hundred thirty-three and thirty-four hundredths

4 four hundred eighty-four and five hundred eleven thousandths

5 eight hundred one and two tenths

6 five hundred sixty-six and two hundred thirteen thousandths

Can Do Spirit!

Helping verbs are used with regular verbs to tell when an action is taking place.

> am   are   is   was   were   will
> has   have   had   shall   should

Terra and Trekk found an article about the Cree Indians, however, it is missing all of the helping verbs. Fill in the blanks using the list and rewrite the story.

The Cree _____ the largest native group in Canada. Their tribe _____ begun in the woodlands around the James Bay. As their population grew they began to spread out across Canada. Groups _____ spreading out throughout Canada to collect more pelts to trade with the European trading posts that _____ been established. They _____ able to gain many things from the Europeans such as new technology. They also acquired horses from them and many tribes moved and settled in the plains. Despite disease and warfare, the Cree _____ able to survive. Today there _____ tribal members that live in reservations in the United States while others _____ been living in the many provinces of Canada. The ancestral language _____ still spoken by many of the elders today.

_____

_____

_____

_____

_____

_____

_____

_____

_____

_____

_____

_____

_____

_____

_____

Friday

What do you think you will have done in a year from now? What places will you have visited? What new friends might you make? How much will you have grown? How well will you have done in the upcoming school year?

_____

_____

_____

_____

_____

_____

_____

_____

_____

_____

_____

_____

_____

_____

_____

_____

Easy "Times"

Multiplying large numbers is easy if they end in zero. Just take the zeros off, multiply, then add the zeros back to the end of your answer.

Here's an example:

4 x 60 = ?

4 x 6 = 24

Now add the zero to the end.
240

Here's another ...

30 x 70 = ?

3 x 7 = 21

Now add the zeros to the end.
2,100

See! It's easy!

Math Races

Get a watch with a second hand. Time yourself doing the first column of problems—as fast as you can! Write your time at the bottom. Remember to multiply the numbers without the zeros and add the zeros back to the result.

Now try the second column. See if you can beat your time.

Race yourself!

		How about a harder race?	
50 x 7 =	5 x 50 =	40 x 500 =	900 x 60 =
40 x 8 =	8 x 90 =	60 x 700 =	50 x 700 =
3 x 90 =	60 x 1 =	200 x 50 =	800 x 30 =
20 x 20 =	40 x 90 =	400 x 80 =	500 x 60 =
80 x 70 =	80 x 10 =	30 x 300 =	80 x 800 =
60 x 60 =	60 x 50 =	200 x 60 =	90 x 400 =
COLUMN 1	COLUMN 2	COLUMN 3	COLUMN 4
TIME:	TIME:	TIME:	TIME:

Will Polar Bears Go With the Floe?

Polar bears hunt ringed seals, their main food, on ice floes. Bears locate holes in the ice by smell, then they catch the seals when they come up for air. As the seasons change, however, and the ice melts, the bears can face lean times because they rarely catch seals in the open water.

In recent years the Arctic Ocean has lost 7% of its ice cover due to climate changes. While bears that live farther north, where it's colder, continue to thrive, bears that live farther south have experienced trouble hunting. Consequently, their numbers have decreased.

Will global warming endanger the polar bears?

Plot this data for the populations of southern and northern polar bears in a line graph to predict the bears' future. Use different colors for the two bear populations.

	Year 1	Year 2	Year 3	Year 4	Year 5	Year 6	Year 7
No. of Southern Bears	3600	3400	3200	3000	2800	2600	2400
No. of Northern Bears	3000	3150	3300	3450	3600	3750	3900

Y-axis: Number of Bears

X-axis: Years

1 2 3 4 5 6 7 8 9 10 11 12 13

Assuming the current rate of decline in Southern Bears, how many bears will there be in year 10? _____

In year 15? _____

In what year will there be no Southern Bears? _____

Assuming Northern Bears continue to increase at their current rate, what will their numbers be in year 14? _____

In year 21? _____

What is the likelihood of Northern Bears becoming extinct? _____

It'll Probably Happen!

Probability is the odds of something happening. If you flip a coin, there is one chance in two that it will land on heads, and one chance in two that it will be tails. These can each be expressed with the ratio 1:2.

Look at the charts below and express the probability as a ratio.
The first one is done for you.

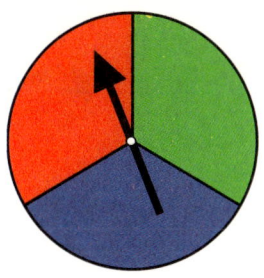

Spinner 1

Spinner 2

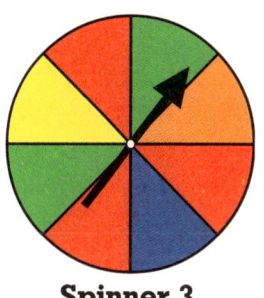

Spinner 3

What is the probability that:

1.) Spinner 1 will land on RED?   1:3

2.) Spinner 1 will land on RED or GREEN?   _____

3.) Spinner 2 will land on RED?   _____

4.) Spinner 2 will land on RED or GREEN?   _____

5.) Spinner 3 will land on RED?   _____

6.) Spinner 3 will land on RED or GREEN?   _____

7.) Spinner 1 will land on RED, GREEN or BLUE?   _____

8.) Spinner 1 will land on BLUE or RED?   _____

9.) Spinner 2 will land on RED, GREEN or BLUE?   _____

10.) Spinner 2 will land on a color with five or more letters in its name? _____

11.) Spinner 2 will land on a color with an "E" in its name?   _____

12.) Spinner 3 will land on a color that there is ONLY ONE of? _____

13.) Spinner 1 will land on GREEN?   _____

14.) Spinner 1 will land on BLUE?   _____

15.) Spinner 2 will land on PURPLE?   _____

16.) Spinner 2 will land on PURPLE or ORANGE?   _____

17.) Spinner 3 will land on GREEN?   _____

18.) Spinner 3 will land on a color with an "O" in its name? _____

More Mega Math

Each of the symbols represents a number between 1 - 10. Can you figure out which number should fill in the blank?

▲■ = ●●●

●●●■ = ●▲▲▲

▲● = _____

NUMBER PUZZLE BOX

Using only the numbers 1 - 9 (and only one time each), fill in the box so that the sum of each row and each column is the same answer.

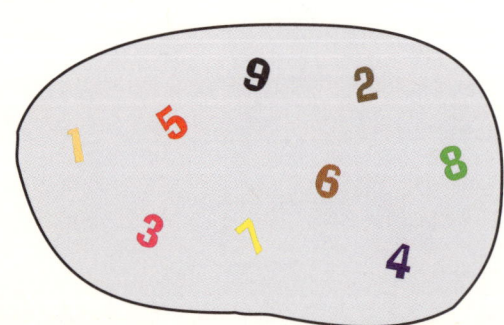

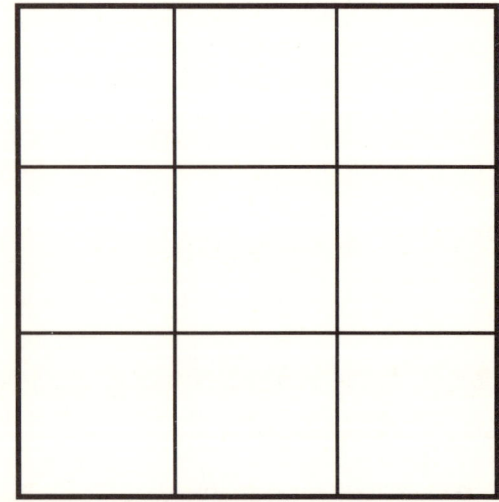

Subject and Predicate

A sentence has two parts—a subject and a predicate. The predicate is the part that says something about the subject.

Circle the predicate in each sentence below.

1 My math book is so heavy.

2 The macaroni and cheese tastes salty.

3 Sara fell on the playground.

4 Bill learned to water ski last summer.

5 Mimi's sunglasses are purple with silver sequins.

6 I baked a chocolate cake today.

7 My dad's car is being repaired.

8 The towel is still wet.

9 I have sand between my toes.

10 Harold played with his nephews.

Hudson's Children

CHAPTER EIGHT

Early the next morning, Terra, Trekk and Trekk's dad went back to work moving the logs, moving the truck, and then repeating the whole process. Trekk could tell that his father was getting concerned. They worked carefully. Trekk's dad shut the truck off and set the brake when they were moving logs, and Trekk and Terra stayed clear whenever the truck moved. The procedure went slowly.

About noon a huge truck roared into the clearing. The three stood and stared as a rough-looking man got down from the driver's seat and walked over.

"'Allo," he said. "I am René. Are you stuck?" The big man spoke with a thick French accent that Terra and Trekk had difficulty understanding. He offered to help, though, and Terra could see that her uncle was glad and relieved.

René first tried driving the truck out himself, but his luck was no better than Trekk's dad's had been. Then Trekk's dad gently drove the truck while René pushed forward and up to keep the wheels from digging in. That didn't work either. "*Quatre*," René grunted. "You need four-wheel drive."

Finally, the big man searched his truck and returned with a long chain. Keeping his own truck on firm ground, he attached the chain to both vehicles. Then he backed almost all the way to the highway, pulling the smaller truck as he went. They were free! Terra, Trekk and Trekk's dad did their best to express their gratitude. They could tell that René understood their English a lot better than they did his French. Finally René waved his hands.

"Do you have anything to drink?" he said. Terra looked at her uncle.

"Uh, just a little soda," he said slowly.

"*Bon*," René said. "Good." They sat and poured a soda into four cups. René made some sort of a toast in French, and then they drank. René laughed, and the others laughed, too. Terra asked him the French words for some common objects.

"Moose," Trekk finally said. "What is moose?"

"Mooooose," René said. Trekk looked at Terra. Could he really be making the same stupid joke as Dad? René laughed. "*Élan,*" he said. He put his hands up to his head like antlers. "*Élan.*"

After shaking hands with them all, René jumped into his big truck and drove away. The campers piled into their truck.

"Interesting man," Trekk's dad said, glancing at the dashboard.

"Hope we make it to a gas station after all this," he added.

"You're kidding, right?" Trekk asked.

"I wish I were," his father answered.

Monday

Activity 8

Skill: Nouns

Across

1. René spoke with this type of an accent.

2. The condition of the campers; rhymes with 2 Down.

3. They toasted with this beverage.

4. Ribbed fabric; with 4 Down, a pioneer "highway."

5. _____, a moose.

Down

1. What spun into the soft surface?

2. Campers' vehicle.

3. What the vehicle was stuck in?

4. With 4 Across, a pioneer "highway."

5. The man who rescued the campers?

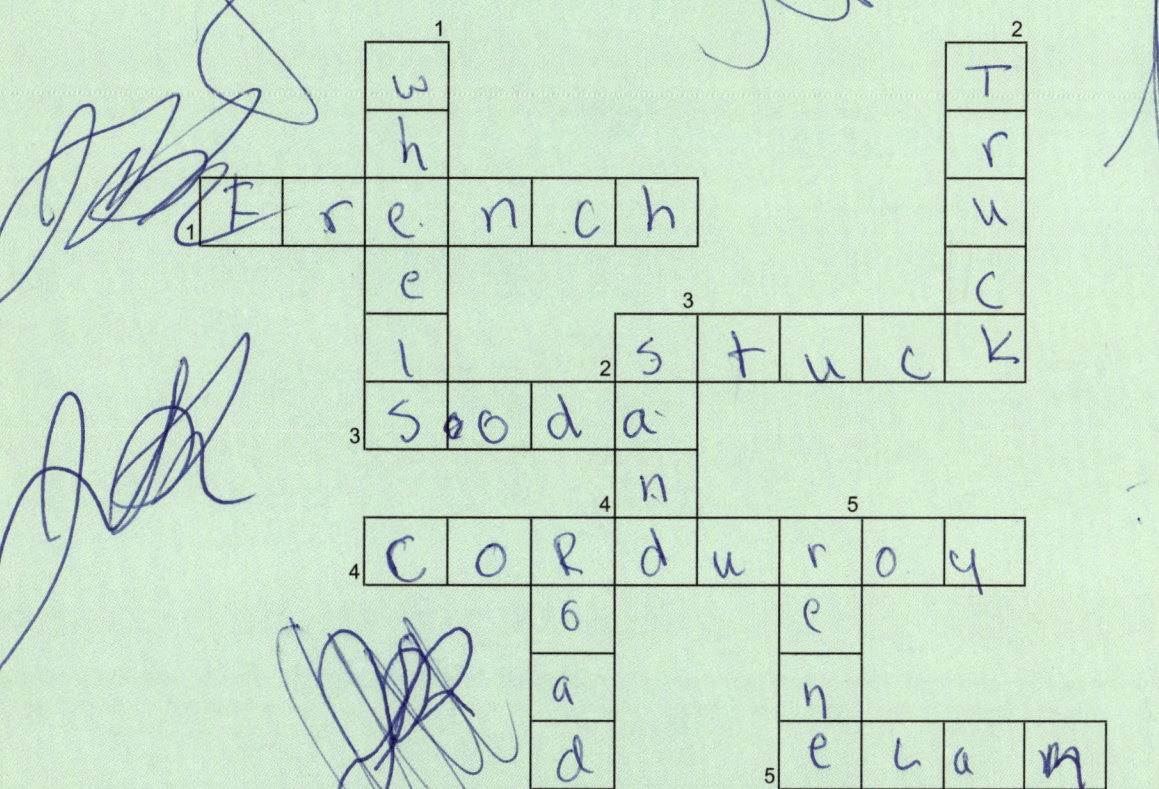

Odd Number Out

Can you figure out which number doesn't belong? Circle the correct answer.

1	82	9	126	45	27
2	8	96	48	12	72
3	72	36	15	6	54

Word Pictures

Can you guess what these mean?

A hop SCOTCH

B MILK — condensed milk

E WALKING — walking on a cloud

F ENVY — green with envy

C BRIDGE water — Bridge over troubled water

G SOUNDSOUNDSOUND — Surround sound

D Banana split

H PLAY PLAY — double play by play

FAMOUS INVENTORS

Match the famous inventors & their inventions.
If you need help, use an encyclopedia or the Internet.

1. An African-American inventor who invented 300 uses for peanuts and developed a revolutionary crop-rotation method.

a. Thomas Alva Edison (1847-1931)

2. Corn flakes

b. Alexander Graham Bell (1847-1922)

3. Bifocals

c. George Washington Carver (1860-1943)

4. The telephone

d. Alfred Nobel (1833-1896)

5. A way to treat milk, for longer storage without it developing microbes (pasteurization).

e. Will Keith Kellogg (1860-1951)

6. Established a prize fund. The prize is awarded annually for achievements in Physics, Chemistry, Physiology or Medicine, Literature and Peace.

f. King C. Gillette (1855-1932)

g. Benjamin Franklin (1706-1790)

7. The light bulb

8. The disposable "safety" razor blade

h. Louis Pasteur (1822-1895)

PERFECT CIRCLES!

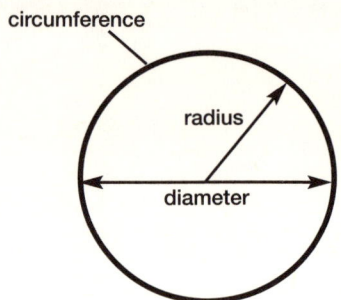

circumference

radius

diameter

When Terra, Trekk and his father came upon a large, circular lake, they began to wonder whether it would be faster to row across if they had a boat, or run around the edge. "The boat would be faster," Trekk said, "because it's shorter."

Trekk's father taught them the formula to find the answer:

1. Multiply the Radius by 2 to figure out the diameter.

2. Multiply the diameter by 3.14 to get a more exact circumference then multiplying by 3.

3. The answer will equal the circumference of that circle.

For example: If the Radius of a circle is 4…

$4 \times 2 = 8$ (8 is the diameter of the circle)

$8 \times 3.14 = 25.12$ (25.12 is the circumference of the circle)

Find the circumference of the following circles using this method and the numbers provided.

1. Radius of 6

Diameter _____   Circumference_____

4. Radius of 12

Diameter _____   Circumference_____

2. Radius of 3.5

Diameter _____   Circumference_____

5. Radius of 2.2

Diameter _____   Circumference_____

3. Radius of 4

Diameter _____   Circumference_____

6. Radius of 8.8

Diameter _____   Circumference_____

What's the circumference of the lake?

Trekk's dad finds out the lake has a radius of three quarters of a mile. What's the diameter and circumference of the lake?

Diameter_____

Circumference_____

Mega Math

Can you solve the following problem? Think about the number of vowels and consonants in each word. Can you detect a rule for solving the unknown amount?

Andy is going camping this weekend. He went to the sporting goods store for supplies. He bought:

- **Granola** $12.00

- **Batteries** $20.00

- **Sleeping Bag**   ?

How much did the sleeping bag cost? What's the rule?

Riddles

1. The first half of me is a popular woman's name. The last half of me is the opposite of sea. There are 49 others like me. What am I?

_____

2. I run, but I never walk. I have a mouth, but I never talk. I have a head, but I never cry. I have a bed, but I never lie. What am I?

_____

3. I am round on both ends and high in the middle. I have two friends that have the same first initial. What state am I?

_____

4. I am the beginning of eternity and the end of time and space, the beginning of every end and the end of every place. What am I?

_____

Thursday

Estimation

Round the numbers in the equations to the nearest hundred and estimate the answer.

Example:
```
      482              500
    x 211            x 200
                 100,000 Estimate
```

1 114
    x 912 ⟶ _____

5 633
    x 747 ⟶ _____

2 452
    x 512 ⟶ _____

6 299
    x 199 ⟶ _____

3 75
    x 142 ⟶ _____

7 387
    x 439 ⟶ _____

4 551
    x 942 ⟶ _____

8 791
    x 829 ⟶ _____

Setting the Scene

Prepositions

At, by, in, on, near, to, from, down, off, through, out, past, up, of, with, for, like, onto, into, about, above, before, behind, below, beside, beneath, between, beyond, during, except, inside, outside, over, upon, without, within

Terra and Trekk discovered an ancient Cree story on how the world began. Exciting and wonderful, the story told of a great flood and how Manobozho helped recreate the world. But the story would not be as wonderful and exciting without prepositional phrases, which tell us when, where, or in what direction something happened. Circle all the prepositional phrases in the story.

One day, Manobozho went out looking for his cousin, but couldn't find him anywhere.

Instead, he saw the trail of a huge snake and he knew that Meshekenabek, the monster snake whose eyes glowed with fire and scales glistened, had kidnapped his cousin. So he followed the trail to the shore of Manitou Lake, where Meshekenabek lived at the bottom all coiled up in a thicket of hissing snakes.

Angry and swearing revenge for his cousin, Manobozho asked the sun to beat down fiercely on the lake. He wanted the lake to get so hot that Meshekenabek would have to crawl out into the shade of the trees along the shore. Manobozho snuck into these trees and hid himself in a tree stump.

The sun heated Manitou Lake until it was boiling hot. Soon, bubbles started coming to the surface. That's when Meshekenabek lifted his head above the water, looking for Manobozho. He saw the tree stump and said, "Aha! Manobozho has disguised himself!"

Hot waves dashed against the rocks as he and the other snakes slithered and slunk toward the shore and the tree stump. One of the snakes wound his tail around the stump and tried to pull it down, but Manobozho held on.

When Meshekenabek crept into the shade to cool down, Manobozho came out of his disguise and shot an arrow at him. Meshekenabek howled with anger! The snakes began to attack Manobozho! The waters of Manitou Lake began to rise so that the whole world began to flood!

Manobozho warned all the people and animals to run. He and all the people and all the animals took refuge on a mountaintop. But the flood continued to rise, so Manobozho built a great raft for all of them. Eventually the water covered the mountaintop, and Manobozho and all the people and all the animals floated for many days.

Can you finish the story? Write down what you think happened.

_____
_____
_____
_____
_____
_____
_____
_____
_____
_____

The real ending is hidden in this book. Look for a clue that tells you where it is.

Friday

Hooray! You just won a million bucks in the lottery! Instead of receiving your winnings in one lump sum, it will be evenly divided over four years. ($250,000 a year.) Describe how you would spend your money for four different years.

_____

_____

_____

_____

_____

_____

_____

_____

_____

_____

_____

_____

_____

_____

_____

_____

_____

_____

The Simple Power of Exponents!

There's an easier way to write some multiplication problems—you just use **exponents**! When you multiply a number by itself—6 x 6—an exponent will make it simpler: 6^2. In this case, 2 is the exponent. It means the same as writing "6 x 6." (And in both cases the answer is 36.)

But the exponent can be a bigger number, like this...4^3.

In this case, 3 is the exponent. It means the same as writing "4 x 4 x 4."

$$4 \times 4 \times 4 =$$
$$(4 \times 4) \times 4 =$$
$$16 \times 4 = 64$$

Rewrite these problems using exponents, then solve...

1. 5 x 5   ___ = _____

2. 8 x 8   ___ = _____

3. 10 x 10   ___ = _____

4. 12 x 12   ___ = _____

5. 36 x 36   ___ = _____

6. 3 x 3 x 3   ___ = _____

7. 10 x 10 x 10   ___ = _____

8. 8 x 8 x 8   ___ = _____

9. 15 x 15 x 15   ___ = _____

10. 7 x 7 x 7 x 7   ___ = _____

11. 10 x 10 x 10 x 10   ___ = _____

12. 2 x 2 x 2 x 2 x 2   ___ = _____

Now try writing out the problem the old way, then solve...
(Use parenthesis to help!)

13. 7^2 _____ = ___

14. 11^2 _____ = ___

15. 16^2 _____ = ___

16. 8^3 _____ = ___

17. 13^3 _____ = ___

18. 3^4 _____ = ___

SPEEDY EXPONENTS!

When we multiply a number by itself many times, we can show this with a multiplication equation.

2 x 2 x 2 x 2 = 16 or we can use an exponent: 2^4 = 16

Solve these exponents! See who's faster, you or a calculator. Solve all the problems and time yourself. Then do them all with a calculator and write down your time.

1. 2^5

2. 10^3

3. 3^3

4. 10^4

5. 4^4

6. 3^5

7. 10^6

8. 3^4

9. 10^5

10. 4^6

My time: _____ Calculator time: _____

And now try these:

11. $10^4 + 2^6 =$

12. $3^2 + 2^3 =$

13. $2^9 + 1^3 =$

14. $2^7 + 7^2 + 10^1 =$

My time: _____ Calculator time: _____

The answer to question 14 is your clue to find the end of the story on page 109.

Metric Road Trip!

Saturday

For measuring, Canada uses the metric system, which is a Base 10 system. That means that every unit of measurement is an exponent of 10.

Meter Reading

1 Kilometer (km)	= 1000 Meters (m)
1 Meter (m)	= 10 Decimeters (dm)
1 Decimeter (dm)	= 10 Centimeters (cm)
1 Centimeter (cm)	= 10 Millimeters (mm)

A kilometer is 1000 meters (or 1×10^3 meters)
It's also 10,000 decimeters (or 1×10^4 decimeters)
It's also 100,000 centimeters (or 1×10^5 centimeters)
It's also 1,000,000 millimeters (or 1×10^6 millimeters)

If you want to convert between metric units, all you do is add or take away zeros. For example, say the distance between two towns is 42 km. That's the same as 42,000 m, 420,000 dm, 4,200,000 cm, and 42,000,000 mm. On the other hand, if the distance between two other towns is 25,000,000 mm, you can easily figure out that it's 2,500,000 cm, 250,000 dm, 25,000 m, and 25 km.

Complete the chart below. Write the answers as both whole numbers and as multiplication problems using exponents.

	Kilometers	Meters	Decimeters	Centimeters	Millimeters
Detroit to Petoskey	362	362×10^3	362×10^4		
		362,000			362,000,000
Petoskey to Moosonee	708			708×10^5	
New York to Detroit					
			8,370,000		
New York to Los Angeles					$4,828 \times 10^6$
Halifax to Vancouver		5,552,000			

More Mega Math

How many triangles add up to 11?

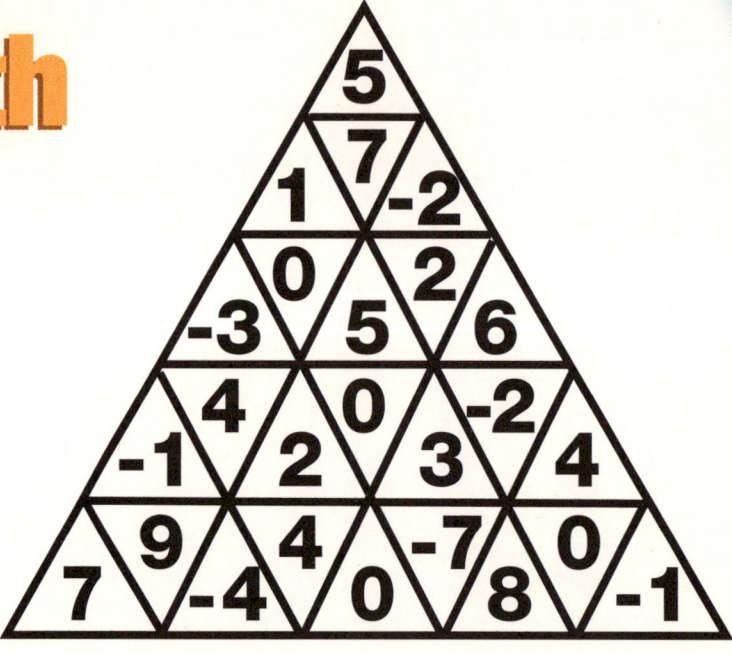

Brain Teaser

Which one doesn't belong?

UNE   AY

            ARCH

EAT   ULY

Division of Fractions

To divide fractions, multiply by a reciprocal, then reduce the fraction to get the answer.

Example: $\dfrac{2}{5} \div \dfrac{9}{10} = \dfrac{2}{5} \times \dfrac{10}{9} = \dfrac{20}{45} = \dfrac{4}{9}$

1. $\dfrac{1}{3} \div \dfrac{2}{3} =$

2. $\dfrac{8}{9} \div \dfrac{5}{7} =$

3. $\dfrac{1}{2} \div \dfrac{5}{6} =$

4. $\dfrac{4}{5} \div \dfrac{3}{7} =$

5. $\dfrac{7}{10} \div \dfrac{1}{4} =$

6. $\dfrac{7}{20} \div \dfrac{1}{5} =$

7. $\dfrac{9}{11} \div \dfrac{1}{11} =$

8. $\dfrac{5}{8} \div \dfrac{3}{4} =$

Hudson's Children

CHAPTER NINE

With the gas gauge nearing E, Trekk's dad told stories and jokes, but the cousins could see him glance often at the sinking pointer. They breathed a sigh of relief when they made it to Hornepayne for gasoline and supplies. Trekk watched the pump run up some amazing numbers before he realized that fuel here was measured in liters, not gallons. Trekk's dad handed him some Canadian bills. "You go and pay."

"A dollar is a dollar, anyway," Trekk said.

"Not quite. Canadian and U.S. currency aren't worth the same amount. Right now, if you exchange ten U.S. dollars, you'll get about fifteen Canadian dollars. The difference depends on the exchange rate, which changes from time to time. Most places accept U.S. dollars, so you have to pay attention to the value."

Refueled and resupplied, the travelers drove on through Hearst and Kapuskasing, hoping to camp that night in René Brunelle Provincial Park. The day was overcast and they thought it might rain, so they made the best time they could. Suddenly Terra yelled, "Stop!"

"What's the matter?" Trekk said. His dad slowed the truck. Terra pointed to a seven-foot-high creature standing at the edge of the woods. "Moose," Trekk breathed.

"*Élan*," Terra whispered. The moose was huge, even from this distance.

"Must be a cow," Trekk's dad said softly. "No antlers."

"Don't bulls lose their antlers sometimes?" Trekk asked.

"In winter," his dad said. "By now they'd be growing back nicely."

"It's graceful somehow," Terra said, "and beautiful."

There was a motion behind the moose, and the cow turned. As she did, they got a glimpse of another, smaller moose just behind. Then in the blink of an eye, both were gone.

"She had a calf with her," Terra said.

"She'll keep it until it's about a year old and then send it on its way. Moose stay pretty solitary except for mating and calf-raising," Trekk's dad said.

It rained the rest of the way to the park, stopping just as they arrived. Hordes of mosquitoes followed and attacked while they set up camp.

"Yipe," Trekk said, "these things are as big as sparrows."

"No, hawks," Terra said, slapping for the hundredth time. It was unbearable. Their repellent didn't do much good. Finally, they fled to the truck, leaving most of their things outside. They had cold beans for dinner and shoved their gear around so that they could fit their sleeping bags on the truck bed.

After sleeping poorly in the cramped truck, they were awakened by loud noises. Trekk tried to see out the truck's rear window. Bulky shapes were moving outside. Someone was stealing their supplies!

Monday

Activity 9

Skill: Vocabulary

Choose the best meaning for each boldfaced word. Circle the letter next to your choice.

1. Canadian and U.S. **currency** aren't worth the same amount.
   a. numbers
   b. fuel
   c. values
   d. money

2. The day was **overcast**.
   a. troubled
   b. cloudy
   c. forgotten
   d. far away

3. They got a **glimpse** of another, smaller moose.
   a. comparison
   b. quick look
   c. noise
   d. scary sight

4. Moose stay pretty **solitary** except for mating and calf-raising.
   a. dangerous
   b. alone
   c. heavy
   d. silent

5. They were attacked by **hordes** of mosquitoes as they set up camp.
   a. sounds
   b. attacks
   c. mobs
   d. stingers

Grid Logic

	Dawn	Lucas	Estaban	Michael	Emma	Metalheads	Stonestown Symphony	Wild Yahoos	Backyard Blues Band	Country Kickin'	Monday	Wednesday	Thursday	Friday	Saturday
Montgomery															
Hawthorne															
Guerro															
Juarez															
Chen															
Monday															
Wednesday															
Thursday															
Friday															
Saturday															
Metalheads															
Stonestown Symphony															
Wild Yahoos															
Backyard Blues Band															
Country Kickin'															

For examples and instructions on how to complete Grid Logic, see the last page of the book.

Five friends went to concerts this past week. Because they all have different tastes in music, they decided to go to five different concerts. All of the concerts were on different days. From the following clues, can you determine each child's full name, the name of the concert they attended, and the day on which the concert was held?

1. Estaban and his friend, the Montgomery girl, both went to concerts before Thursday.

2. The Chen boy saw the Metalheads later in the week than Michael saw his concert.

3. Country Kickin' played a concert earlier in the week than the Wild Yahoos, who Dawn saw in concert.

4. The Hawthorne girl, Dawn, and the child who went to Friday's concert all ride the same bus to school.

5. Backyard Blues Band played on Thursday, three days after the Guerro child went to his concert.

6. Estaban saw his concert before the Chen child and five days before the girl who saw Stonestown Symphony.

TAKE ME TO YOUR LEADER

Match the planets to their descriptions. If you need help,
use an encyclopedia or the Internet.

1. Mercury

2. Jupiter

3. Pluto

4. Venus

5. Saturn

6. Mars

7. Uranus

8. Neptune

a. The God of War,
   Red Planet   Aires

b. The Magician, father of
   Saturn

c. Goddess of Love and
   Beauty, the "morning star"

d. God of Agriculture,
   ringed planet

e. God of the Underworld,
   not a dog

f. Winged Messenger of
   the gods

g. God of the Sea, in Greek
   it's Poseidon

h. King of the gods,
   Great Red Spot

119

SKATE MONSTER 360S!

Trekk's plan to master 360s on his skateboard is going well. He's almost there, but he wants to try a few other kids' skateboards, which are different sizes. Help him calculate the angle, diameter, and circumference of his attempts.

Example:

radius x 2 = diameter   37" x 2 = 74"

diameter x 3.14 = circumference   74" x 3.14 = 232.36"

360° – angle 1 = angle 2   360° – 102° = 258°

1.

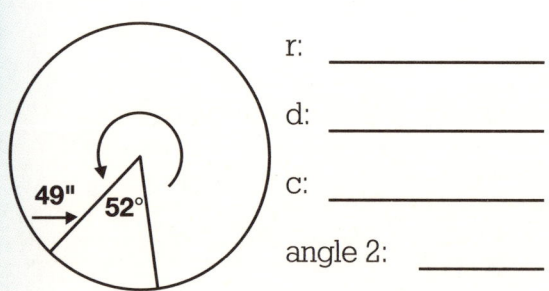

r: _____

d: _____

c: _____

angle 2: _____

2.

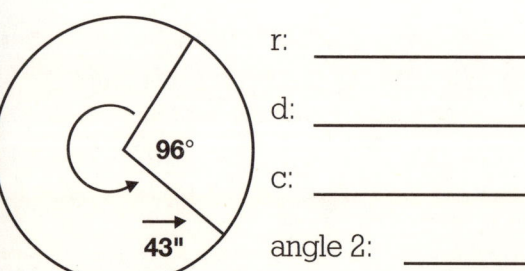

r: _____

d: _____

c: _____

angle 2: _____

4.

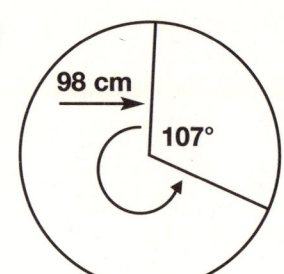

r: _____

d: _____

c: _____

angle 2: _____

3.

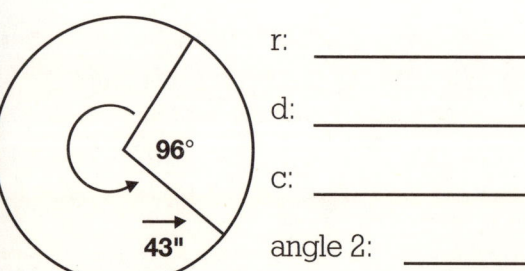

r: _____

d: _____

c: _____

angle 2: _____

5.

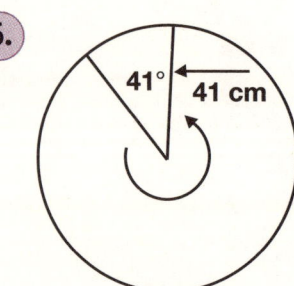

r: _____

d: _____

c: _____

angle 2: _____

Mega Math

Use $1 bills, $5 bills, $10 bills, $20 bills and $50 bills to solve this problem.

James was saving his money to buy a new pair of skis. So far he has saved $340.00 made up of an equal number of four different bills. Which four bills did he have? How many of each?

Riddles

1 I am at my peak when I am round, but I am often seen in other shapes. A man whose last name means "powerful bicep" was the first human to walk on me. I come out at night but sometimes you may catch a glimpse of me in the daytime. What am I?

_____

2 I am weightless and can be seen. When I am put in a barrel I make it lighter. What am I?

_____

Thursday

Read the Graph

Annual Grocery Spending for Jones Family
Examine the graph to answer the questions below.

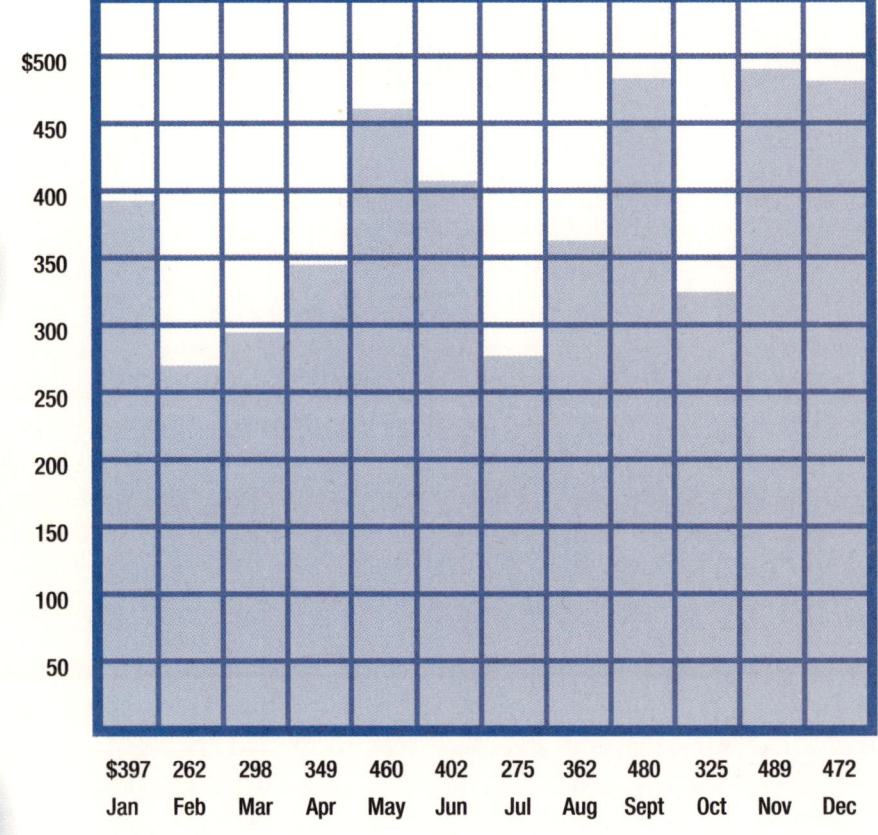

	$500											
	450											
	400											
	350											
	300											
	250											
	200											
	150											
	100											
	50											

$397	262	298	349	460	402	275	362	480	325	489	472
Jan	Feb	Mar	Apr	May	Jun	Jul	Aug	Sept	Oct	Nov	Dec

1. In what month did the Jones family spend the most money?

_____

2. In what month did the Jones family spend the least money?

_____

3. What is the difference between the greatest and least amount of spending?

_____

4. What is the monthly spending average? Remember, to calculate average
you add the totals for each month and divide by the total number of months.

_____

Don't Be Negative!

Terra is reading the diary of the wife of a trader who worked for the Hudson's Bay Company. During that time, many men married the women of the tribes they traded furs with. Marrying Native women was beneficial because they could better adapt to the environment and had skills that helped them in survival. There are many grammatical errors in this journal because the native language that she spoke was recorded in French and then translated into English. One common error in this diary is the use of *double negatives*. A *double negative* is the use of two negatives so that they cancel each other out.

Find the double negatives in the journal entry below and underline them.

My husband is a voyageur working for the Hudson's Bay Company. I hardly have no time to spend with him because there always isn't no time. He is so busy establishing posts along the James Bay and Hudson Bay. My husband don't catch no animals. Members of other tribes bring in the furs and trade them for goods. The tribes need items made of metal like knives and weapons since they don't have no way of making it themselves. This sure ain't no good way to work. They ain't going to be no help to themselves. There just isn't no good that will come of it.

Now rewrite the journal correctly.

_____

_____

_____

_____

_____

_____

_____

_____

_____

_____

Friday

Surprise! You just won a gift certificate for a brand new Apricot computer. The computer company will design it to fit your specific needs. Describe everything you want your computer to do.

_____
_____
_____
_____
_____
_____
_____
_____
_____
_____
_____
_____
_____
_____
_____
_____
_____
_____

Please Excuse My Dear Aunt Sally!

Use this sentence—"Please Excuse My Dear Aunt Sally"—
to remember the order of operations.

Please	=	Parentheses	$4 - 3 \times 2 \div (14 - 12) + 2^2 \times 3 - 1 = ?$
Excuse	=	Exponents	$4 - 3 \times 2 \div 2 + 2^2 \times 3 - 1 = ?$
My	=	Multiplication	$4 - 3 \times 2 \div 2 + 4 \times 3 - 1 = ?$
Dear	=	Division	$4 - 6 \div 2 + 12 - 1 = ?$
Aunt Sally	=	Addition & Subtraction	$4 - 3 + 12 - 1 = ?$
			$1 + 12 - 1 = ?$
			$13 - 1 = 12$

Addition and subtraction should be done in order across the problem.

Solve the following problems:

1.) $3 + 7 \times 4 - 2 (2 \times 5) + 2 + 3^2 =$ _____

2.) $4^2 \times 2 - 2 \times (4^2 + 4 - 4) =$ _____

3.) $7 + 2^2 - (2 \times 3) + (3+1)^2 - 4 \times 2 =$ _____

4.) $9^2 - (2+6)^2 \div 8 \times (0+2) - 4 =$ _____

5.) $(2 + 9)^2 - 2 + (10 \div 2) + 5 + 3 \times (2 + 1)^2 =$ _____

6.) $(4 \times 5) + (2 \times 4)^2 - 3^2 \times (3 \times 4 - 3) =$ _____

7.) $3^2 - (4^2 \times 4) \div 8 + 1 =$ _____

8.) $(3 \times 4)^2 + 2 \times (2 + 3)^2 - 4 \times (3 \times 4^2) =$ _____

9.) $8 \times 4 + 2 - 7 \times 3 + 12 \div 3 - 9 + 7 \times 8 \div 4 =$ _____

10.) $6 \div (6 - 4) + (4 \times 2) - (3^2 + 2) =$ _____

11.) $8 + 82 - (8 \times 8) + 8 =$ _____

12.) $(22 \times 4) + 6 - 8 + 10 =$ _____

13.) $10 \times 9 + 8 - 7 + (6 - 2)^2 =$ _____

14.) $2 + 22 \times 2 - 2 \div 2 =$ _____

Predators Gone Wild

Predators usually hunt plant-eating animals, such as deer and rabbits. Without predators, these animals could eat so many plants that none of them would have enough food. When predators hunt the weak animals, they keep the prey animal population at a sustainable level.

Because predators depend on the availability of prey to survive, it's vital that a certain proportion (or ratio) of prey exist relative to the number of predators. For example, if each polar bear needs 5 seals to survive the season, the ratio must be 1 : 5 (or higher).

Owls live on mice. Suppose that the ideal ratio of mice to owls is 10:1. Solve the equations and calculate the ratio for each scenario using the chart below. Decide if the owls will go hungry or survive. (Remember: $10^1 = 10$, $10^2 = 100$.)

Forest	Mice	Owls	Ratio	Prediction
A. 4×10^1 mice, 2×10^1 owls	40	20	2:1	Go Hungry
B. 9×10^1 mice, 2×10^1 owls				
C. 16×10^2 mice, 1×10^2 owls				
D. 12×10^4 mice, 12×10^3 owls				
E. 14×10^2 mice, 7×10^1 owls				
F. 21×10^2 mice, 3×10^2 owls				
G. 6×10^2 mice, 4×10^1 owls				
H. 3×10^3 mice, 3×10^1 owls				
I. 7×10^4 mice, 8×10^3 owls				
J. 8×10^4 mice, 4×10^2 owls				
K. 5×10^3 mice, 5×10^2 owls				
L. 3×10^3 mice, 7×10^2 owls				

Hunting with the Lynx!

The Canadian lynx is an elusive wild cat that hunts snowshoe hare in the boreal forests of Canada, Michigan, Wisconsin, and Minnesota. You remember from page 29 that every ecosystem has a delicate balance of consumers and producers. On the average, each lynx consumes about 200 snowshoe hare every year.

Let's study the Canadian lynx. We have gathered some data for British Columbia where the proportion of lynx to hare has remained constant over a 50-year period at a 1:250 ratio. In the chart at the right, calculate the number of hare for each year if every year the ratio of lynx to hare is 1:250. For instance, if there are 79 lynx, then there has to be 79 x 250 or 19,750 hare.

Year	# of Lynx (in thousands)	# of Hare (in thousands)
1950	79	
1955	41	
1960	160	
1965	37	
1970	100	
1975	12	
1980	140	
1985	21	
1990	90	
1995	14	

Range

First, let's calculate the *average* number of lynx over the past fifty years and the average number of snowshoe hare.

Average number of lynx   1950-1995 _____

Average number of hare   1950-1995 _____

The *range* of numbers is the spread from the lowest number to the highest. For our Canadian lynx, the lowest number was 12 and the highest was 160, so the range was 12-160.

Find the range for the number of lynx and hare over the past 50 years.

Range of lynx   1950-1995 _____   Range of hare   1950-1995 _____

What's the relationship of average to the range in our populations? Is it exactly in the middle?

More Mega Math

Each of the symbols represents a number between 1 - 10. Can you figure out which number should fill in the blank?

Number Puzzle Box

Now try this Number Puzzle Box using only the numbers 1 - 16 (once each). (Here's a hint: The sum of each column and row is 34.)

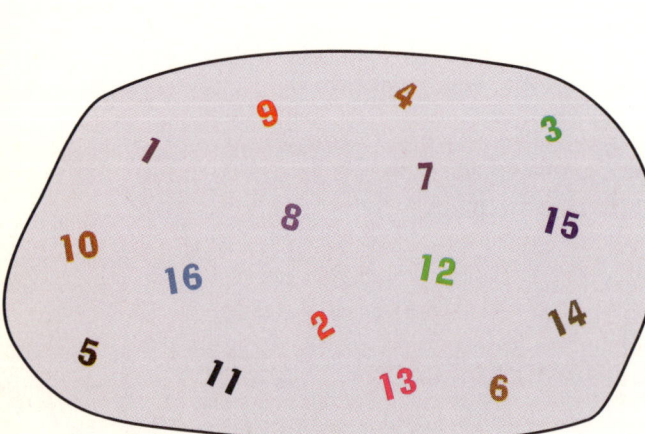

Math Quiz

Select the correct answer for each problem.

1 Which equation equals 60?

A. 5 x (10 x 2)

B. (12 x 4) − 6

C. (8 + 4) x 5

D. 6 x (12 ÷ 4)

2 Which fraction is equivalent to $\frac{2}{3}$?

A. $\frac{16}{19}$

B. $\frac{8}{12}$

C. $\frac{5}{6}$

D. $\frac{6}{14}$

3 Which decimal is equivalent to $\frac{82}{10,000}$?

A. .0082

B. .082

C. .82

D. .00082

4 What number represents the shaded figures below?

A. $1\frac{1}{3}$

B. $1\frac{1}{2}$

C. $1\frac{5}{9}$

D. $\frac{15}{9}$

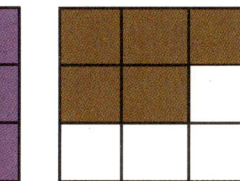

Hudson's Children

CHAPTER TEN

Terra fumbled around for a flashlight. Her uncle and Trekk crawled over each other, trying to get a better look at what was happening outside. Finally Terra found the light, turned it on, and aimed it through the window. "Bears!" Trekk shouted. Attracted by what the campers had left outside, the bears were trashing the camp. Trekk's dad took the light and lifted the rear window so he could see better. There appeared to be three of them, possibly a mother and two cubs. The bears made no effort to flee. "Shoo!" Trekk's dad yelled, and waved the beam over their faces.

"Go!" shouted Trekk. One bear half rose to look in the direction of the noise, but the light didn't seem to bother any of them.

"Shoo!" Trekk's dad yelled even louder. He stuck his arm out the rear window and pounded on the tailgate of the truck. "Get out of here!" Suddenly there was a loud metallic bang, and the whole truck shook. Terra and Trekk fell, and Trekk's dad dropped the flashlight out and let go

of the window at the same time. One of the bears hit the truck. They could hear the bear scratch the side of the bed and then hit it again. For a moment, the frightened trio thought the bears were trying to get inside. The three cowered in the truck's darkness. There was nothing to be done. After a while, it grew completely silent. They strained their eyes looking and saw nothing, but no one was tempted to go out to retrieve the flashlight, let alone look for bears.

In the gray light of dawn, the campers checked the damage. Everything in the cooler was gone or ruined. The cooler itself was destroyed, and the water jug was punctured. The side of the truck had a small dent, and there were scratches on the bed rail. "I guess I'll owe Jim some repair costs," Trekk's dad said. "Let's get this mess cleaned up before the bugs find us."

"Too late," Trekk said. "The mosquito squadron has located its target." They worked quickly to pick up the campsite, hurried by the whine of insect wings. There was nothing to do but resupply.

"We can go on to Cochrane," Trekk's dad said. "That's it anyway. There are no more roads from there. We have to go north another way."

Visions of dogsleds danced in Trekk's head, but it was July. "So now what?"

"Polar Bear Express," his dad said.

"The what?" Terra asked.

"The Polar Bear Express," her uncle replied.

"Thank you," Terra said as she stuffed the useless water jug into a trash bag, "but I've had enough bears for now."

The way north was by rail.

Monday

Activity 10

Skill: Compound Sentences

Write a sentence to answer each
of the following questions.

1. What did Terra do when she found the flashlight?

   _____

   _____

   _____

2. What did Trekk's dad do first when he took the flashlight?

   _____

   _____

3. How did Trekk's dad try to scare off the bears?

   _____

   _____

4. How did the bears react to Trekk's dad pounding on the truck?

   _____

   _____

5. What was the condition of the truck in the morning?

   _____

   _____

6. What was the condition of their equipment in the morning?

   _____

   _____

Funny Alphabet!

Let's have some fun with alliteration. Alliteration is when you combine words with the same first letter or sound in a phrase or sentence. . . Try it! (Use a dictionary if you get stuck.)

A is an angry alligator that ate an awful apple.

B is a big, brown bear that... _____

C is a _____

D is a _____

E is an _____

F is a _____

G is a _____

H is a _____

I is an _____

J is a _____

K is a _____

L is a _____

M is a _____

N is a _____

O is an _____

P is a _____

Q is a _____

R is a _____

S is a _____

T is a _____

U is an _____

V is a _____

W is a _____

Y is a _____

Z is a _____

ELEMENTARY, MY DEAR

Match the elements to their periodic symbols and hints.
If you need help, use an encyclopedia or the Internet.

1. gold

2. silver

3. copper

4. iron

5. mercury

6. platinum

7. tin

8. lead

a. Sn, asked the wizard for a heart

b. Pt, high record sales

c. Pb, Superman can't see through it

d. Au, caused miners quite a rush

e. Cu, plumbing fixtures

f. Hg, slippery liquid

g. Fe, important in the blood

h. Ag, the Lone Ranger's horse

ALL BOXED IN! Wednesday

A three-dimensional rectangle has six sides or FACES. To find the total surface area, you must compute the area for each surface, then add them up. However, since each face has the same area as its OPPOSITE SIDE, you only need to compute THREE SIDES, multiply each number by 2, then add them up. Use "Please Excuse My Dear Aunt Sally" to help you!

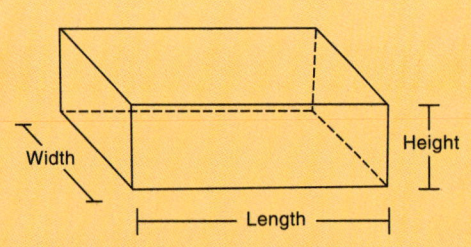 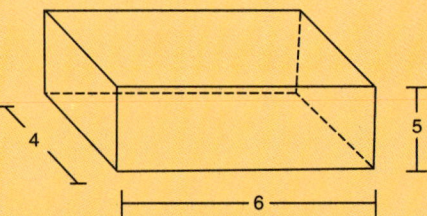

Use this formula:

2 x (L x W) + 2 x (W x H) + 2 x (H x L) =
Total Surface Area

Here's an example:

2 x (6 x 4) + 2 x (4 x 5) + 2 x (5 x 6) = ?
2 x (24) + 2 x (20) + 2 x (30) = ?
48 + 40 + 60 = 148

Find the areas for the following three-dimensional rectangles.

1.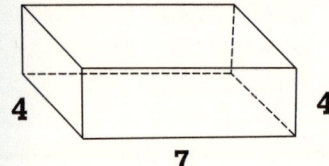

2.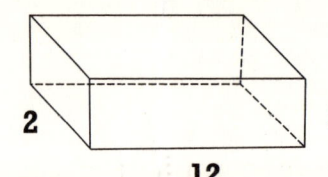

3.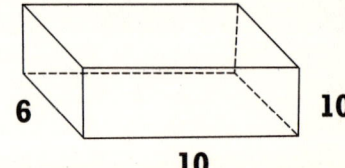

4.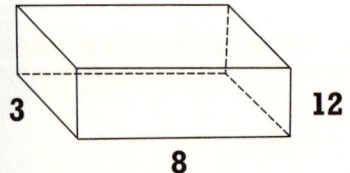

5.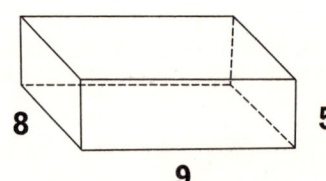

6.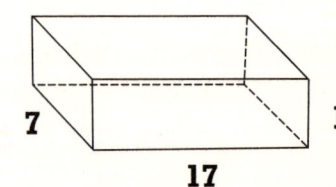

7. L = 15, W = 5, H = 25

8. L = 10, W = 4, H = 14

9. L = 14, W = 13, H = 12

Mega Math

Can you solve the following problem? Assign different values for consonants and vowels. Can you detect a rule for solving the unknown amount?

Christi and her friend Jenna went to the mall for new clothes. They bought the following items:

- Jeans $22.00

- Shirts $18.00

- Wool Sweater   ?

How much did the wool sweater cost? What's the rule?

Riddles

1 The last four letters of me are one of a connected series. I am an action that protects while it cleanses. My last three letters can be found in the newspaper. What am I?

_____

2 I am an insect but you might find another insect in my name. A very recognizable band was once named after me. What am I?

_____

Word Pictures

Can you guess what these mean?

A 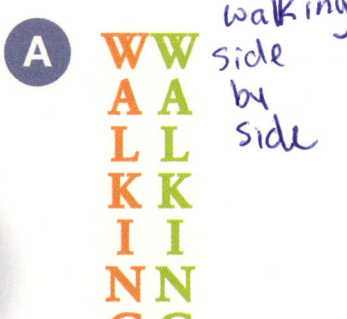 walking side by side

D  eating on the run

F  down under

B 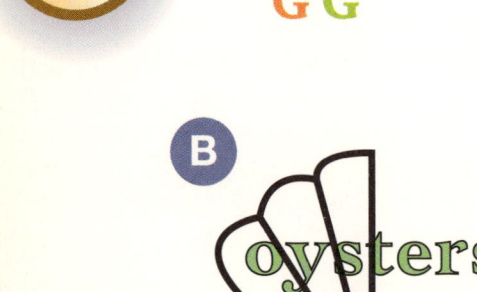  oysters in a shell

E  once upon a time

G  heart broken

C  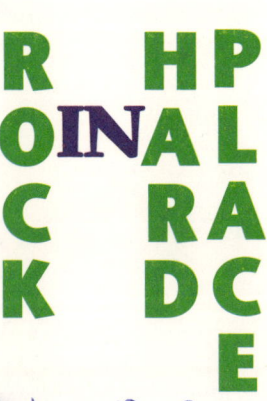 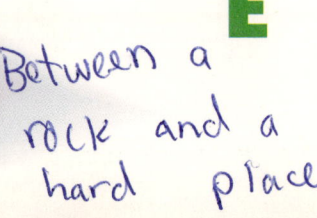 Between a rock and a hard place

H   down town

Exciting Adverbs

An *adverb* helps to describe a verb, an adjective or another adverb. Adverbs help to explain when, where, why, how and to what extent.

Read the antique advertisements below and rewrite them including adverbs. Choose adverbs from the list on the right or come up with your own!

THE WORLD'S GREATEST TALKING MACHINE!

You can _____ make $25.00 in an evening giving public exhibitions in halls and churches! The new Gem Gramophone, or talking machine, reproduces sound so _____, _____, and _____ that even the speaker's own mother can't tell the difference!

WORLD'S FINEST MECHANICAL CALCULATING MACHINE!

You can _____ find the sum and difference of numbers by _____ turning the crank handle. The crank handle _____ rotates all the pinwheels and moves the attached levers. Multiplication can be done by _____ turning the handle to add the same number to the accumulator!

Now it's your turn!
Write an advertisement describing computers and what they are used for. Come up with a creative title, and don't forget to include adverbs in your description!

_____

_____

_____

_____

_____

_____

_____

_____

_____

Friday

Some people are very skilled when it comes to creating things such as chairs, sofas, electronics, etc. If you could create an object or something useful, what would it be? What kind of training would you need to do it?

_____

_____

_____

_____

_____

_____

_____

_____

_____

_____

_____

_____

_____

_____

_____

_____

_____

Very Able with Variables

At a store in Cochrane, Terra wanted a large pack of bubble gum but didn't have the $1.00 it cost. Trekk was willing to lend her the dollar, but he also wanted a 60¢ candy bar.

$$\$.60 + \$1.00 = \$1.60$$

But what if Trekk wanted to buy more candy bars? He knew it would be something like...

(the number of candy bars times $.60) + $1.00 = the total cost

Because the number of candy bars that Trekk could buy can change (or vary), we call it a VARIABLE. In algebra, we use letters to stand for variables. If X is the amount of candy bars, then...

(X times $.60) + $1.00 = the total cost

If the amount of candy bars changes, then it only makes sense for the total cost to change too. We use a second variable, Y, to represent the total cost:

$$(X \times \$0.60) + \$1.00 = Y$$

Using this formula, figure out the total cost if Trekk buys the following number of candy bars and gives Terra $1.00:

1. 1   (1 x $.60) + $1.00 = Y   Y = $1.60

2. 2   _____

3. 5   _____

4. 10   _____

5. 12   _____

6. 18   _____

7. 20   _____

Suppose Trekk has only so much money to spend. Use the formula to calculate how many candy bars he can buy if he has:

8. $2.80   (X x $.60) + $1.00 = $2.80 $2.80 − $1.00 = $1.80 $1.80 ÷ $.60 = 3

9. $5.80   _____

10. $6.40   _____

11. $10.00   _____

12. $11.20   _____

13. $13.00   _____

14. $14.50   _____

Planting New Seeds

When Terra and Trekk neared Hudson Bay, they were surprised that there were so few trees. The Hudson Plains is a transition zone between the Boreal Shield and the tundra. Some trees, like spruce and tamarack, grow, but tundra plants, like sedge and cottongrass, cover the ground near the coast.

Most tundra plants are unique. They must endure wind, soil disturbed by frost, low light, and long hours of sun during the summer. Most of them are "cushion plants" that grow flat on the ground to withstand the wind. These plants feed geese and migratory birds in the summer, and caribou and other animals during the rest of the year.

This flat, open land can be easily damaged. Global warming, along with an overpopulation of snow geese, threatens the tundra plants. Geese eat the plants' roots, so that the plants can't grow back. Without plants to hold the soil in place and insulate it, the ground warms more quickly. When the permafrost, or frozen subsoil, melts, the ground collapses. Scientists estimate that nearly one third of the habitat has been destroyed and another third has been damaged along Hudson Bay's western coast.

To save these special plants, the areas in which these plants grow is protected, and scientists collect seeds and work to rehabilitate the damaged areas, so that all the animals can have enough to eat.

Match the Facts

Match the item in the left column with a description in the right column.

_____ **1.** permafrost   **a.** common tundra plants

_____ **2.** cushion plants   **b.** overpopulated species that eats tundra plants

_____ **3.** spruce and tamarack   **c.** frozen subsoil

_____ **4.** snow geese   **d.** one important cause of damage to tundra plants

_____ **5.** global warming   **e.** trees that grow on the Hudson Plains

_____ **6.** sedge and cottongrass   **f.** low plants that grow flat against the ground

_____ **7.** transition zone   **g.** plants can't grow back

_____ **8.** ground collapse   **h.** role of Hudson Plains

_____ **9.** loss of plant roots   **i.** hold soil in place

_____ **10.** plants   **j.** caused by melting permafrost

Too Many Geese!

Due to warmer and rich farmlands, the lesser snow goose population has tripled in 20 years and continues to grow. There are now more than 4.5 million adult birds. Every summer, they nest in the fragile coastal wetlands ecosystem of the Hudson Plains, where there aren't enough plants to feed them all.

How can the geese and plants be saved? You can help out.

Starting with 4.5 million birds, calculate how many birds there will be if the population goes up 5% every year for the next 5 years. Plot this on the graph below. (Hint: To calculate each year's population, multiply the previous year's population by 1.05.)

Year 1 __4,500,000__ geese

Year 2 _____ geese

Year 3 _____ geese

Year 4 _____ geese

Year 5 _____ geese

Y-axis:

_____

_____

Year 1　Year 2　Year 3　Year 4　Year 5

X-axis: _____

If wildlife managers and farmers use a variety of strategies to limit the birds' food and breeding, they might instead reduce the population by 8% per year. Starting at 4.5 million birds, calculate the number of geese every year for the next 5 years. Plot this on the graph, but in a different color. (Hint: To calculate each year's population, multiply the previous year's population by 0.92.)

Year 1 __4,500,000__ geese

Year 2 _____ geese

Year 3 _____ geese

Year 4 _____ geese

Year 5 _____ geese

Odd Number Out

Can you figure out which fraction doesn't belong?

1 $\dfrac{18}{54}$ $\dfrac{13}{39}$ $\dfrac{26}{78}$ $\dfrac{4}{12}$ $\dfrac{6}{27}$

2 $\dfrac{4}{16}$ $\dfrac{12}{48}$ $\dfrac{28}{112}$ $\dfrac{24}{100}$ $\dfrac{20}{80}$

3 $\dfrac{6}{36}$ $\dfrac{48}{288}$ $\dfrac{12}{72}$ $\dfrac{18}{108}$ $\dfrac{30}{211}$

Cause and Effect

Record the cause and effect for each statement below:

1 Sam couldn't watch television for one week because he failed his science test.

Cause: Sam failed his science test.

Effect: Sam couldn't watch television for a week.

2 Ellen made a get-well card for her grandma who was very sick.

Cause: _____

Effect: _____

3 Rick's hair was hanging in his eyes, so he got a haircut.

Cause: _____

Effect: _____

4 Amber loved to draw so her mom got her art lessons for her birthday.

Cause: _____

Effect: _____

Optical Illusions

There are two women here. Can you find both the old woman and the young one?

Which way do you see the arrows pointing?

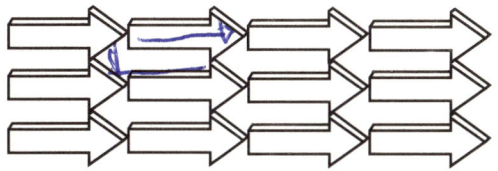

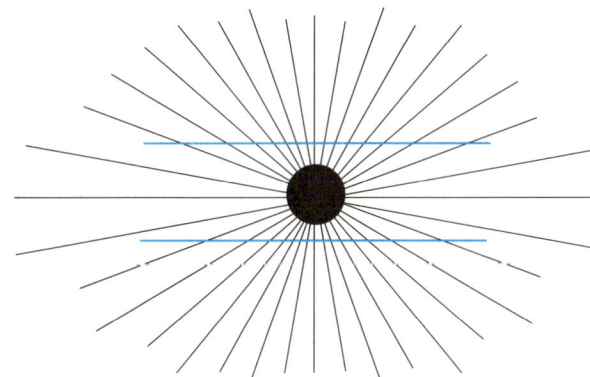

Are the blue lines straight or bent?

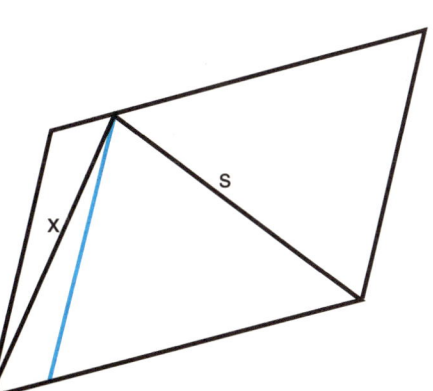

Which line is longer, x or s?

Hudson's Children

CHAPTER ELEVEN

The three travelers were unable to get tickets for the Polar Bear Express. This popular and luxurious train was fully booked by tourist groups. "I'm sorry," Trekk's dad said. "I've heard that this is one of last great rail trips in the world." He looked depressed.

"Maybe we can wait for the next one?" Trekk asked.

"Good plan," Terra said.

"You know, that gives me an idea," her uncle said. "Hang on." Terra's uncle returned, beaming. He had gotten seats on the Little Bear, the year-round regular train to Moosonee and James Bay. The Little Bear was not intended for tourists. It left later and took longer than the Polar Express, and it didn't make a round-trip on the same day, as the Polar Express did. Miraculously, Trekk's dad had also found lodging in Moosonee. They would leave on Friday and return on Saturday.

Trekk and Terra had ridden only metro trains in cities and were very excited. They got to watch the train connect passenger cars, freight cars, and flat cars. Their car didn't have the luxury of the Polar Bear Express, but it seemed more adventurous.

The train went north past the Abitibi River, once a highway of the fur trade. Then it slowed and stopped.

"Don't tell me the train got stuck," Trekk said.

"No, it's just picking up passengers," his dad said.

"I don't see any station here," Terra noted.

"The Little Bear is one of the last flag-stop trains in Canada. The train stops whenever someone flags it down. There are no roads up here, so it's the only way to go." Trekk and Terra craned their heads around to see a local family boarding.

The train made several such stops, and the 186 miles to Moosonee took nearly five hours. Along the way, they passed spruce forests, a giant hydroelectric dam, the great Moose River, and the prehistoric beaches of James Bay, or the inlet that drops down from Hudson Bay.

Moosonee was a bustling town. Still, the town maintained its sense of the past. The travelers took a "water taxi," or motorized canoe, to the town of Moose Factory, the oldest town in Ontario. There they saw Cree people living and working as they had for centuries, and they saw the restored buildings of the Hudson Bay Company, whose trading helped develop North America.

"Is this it, Dad?" Trekk asked. "Is this what you want to write about?"

"I don't have an idea yet," Trekk's dad admitted. "Can you think of something?" They spent the rest of the day taking in the frontier atmosphere.

As they boarded the train the next day, Trekk said, "Tell us more about Henry Hudson."

"It's not a happy ending, I'm afraid."

"Tell us anyway," Terra insisted.

Monday

Activity 11

Skill: Passage Comprehension

Match the item in the left column with a description from the right column.

_____ 1. Polar Bear Express

    a. oldest town in Ontario

_____ 2. Abitibi

    b. inlet that drops down from Hudson Bay

_____ 3. Little Bear

    c. motorized canoe

_____ 4. water taxi

    d. bay named for an explorer

_____ 5. Hudson Bay

    e. year-round transport to Moosonee and James Bay

_____ 6. flag stop

    f. river used by fur traders

_____ 7. James Bay

    g. luxurious nonstop train to Moosonee

_____ 8. Moose Factory

    h. unscheduled pickup of passengers

Math Maze

Circle With the Same Answer

- Using six different numbers inside of the circle, find the two separate equations that reach the total of "180."

- You can only use multiplication and division in your equations, either dividing your numbers then multiplying your total by another number or vice versa.

- Remember, you are only using three numbers from the circle per equation, for a total of six. And your two answers must both equal 180.

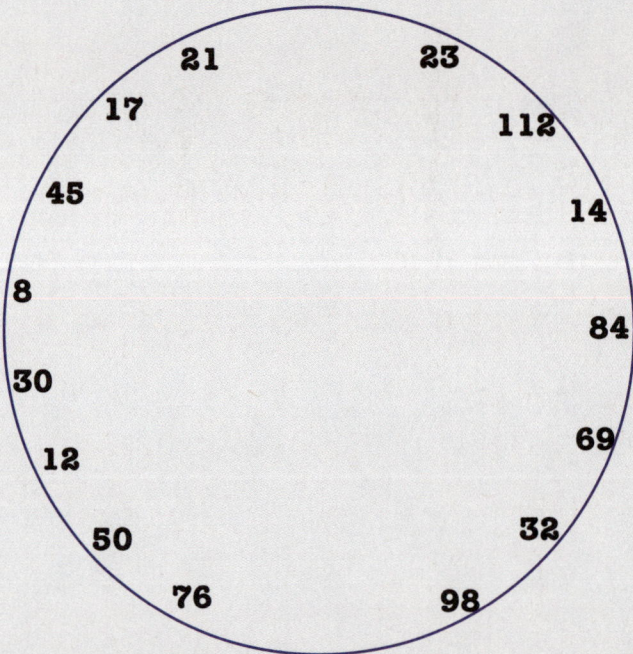

21   23
17   112
45   14
8   84
30
12   69
50   32
76   98

Antonyms, Synonyms or Homonyms

Antonyms mean the opposite. Synonyms mean the same. Homonyms sound alike but mean different. Identify the relationship for the words below.

1. reflect   think   _____
2. overcome   succumb   _____
3. course   coarse   _____
4. capital   capitol   _____
5. adviser   mentor   _____
6. casual   formal   _____

CATCH-22

Match the phrases to their meanings. If you need help, use an encyclopedia or the Internet.

1. push the envelope

a. to annoy to the point of frustration

2. cold turkey

b. in a difficult position

3. by the skin of one's teeth

c. dressed very elegantly

4. cut and dried

d. to view something with skepticism

5. dressed to the nines

e. to go beyond the known safe limits

6. get one's goat

f. a very narrow escape

7. grain of salt

g. to quit an addictive habit suddenly

8. rock and a hard place

h. routine, ordinary, obvious

FRIGHTENING FREIGHT

While waiting for the Little Bear train, Trekk and Terra watched trains link up along the tracks. Terra said, "I wonder how much stuff is in those box cars." "Wait, I learned that last year," Trekk said. "The formula for the volume of a box is Length x Width x Height = Volume." Terra traced numbers in the air. "So if that box car measures 20 meters x 7.5 meters x 5 meters, then the volume is 750 cubic meters."

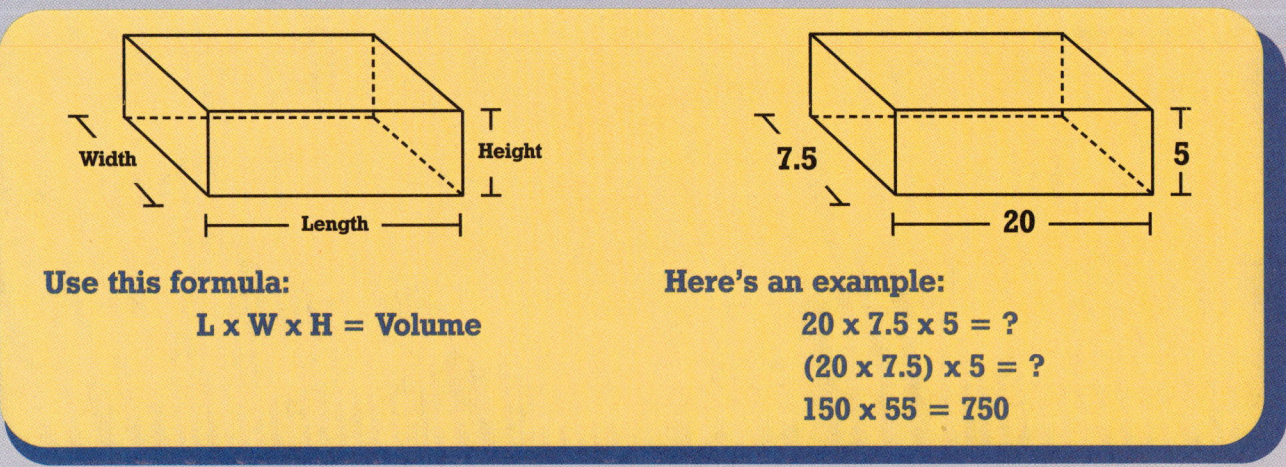

Use this formula:

$$L \times W \times H = Volume$$

Here's an example:

$$20 \times 7.5 \times 5 = ?$$
$$(20 \times 7.5) \times 5 = ?$$
$$150 \times 55 = 750$$

Using the formula above, find the volume of each of these box cars.

1.

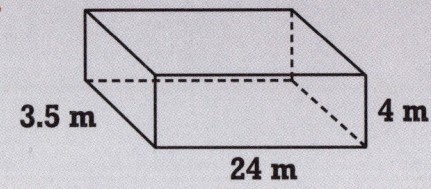

3.5 m   4 m   24 m

2.

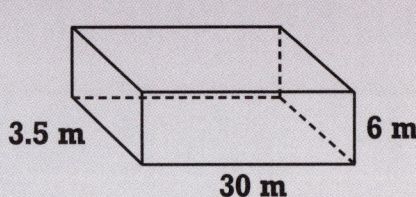

3.5 m   6 m   30 m

3. $20 \text{ m} \times 3.5 \text{ m} \times 5 \text{ m} =$

4. $13 \text{ m} \times 3.5 \text{ m} \times 4 \text{ m} =$

5. $17 \text{ m} \times 3.5 \text{ m} \times 6 \text{ m} =$

6. $22 \text{ m} \times 3.5 \text{ m} \times 5 \text{ m} =$

7. $14 \text{ m} \times 3.5 \text{ m} \times 4 \text{ m} =$

Mega Math

Use $1 bills, $5 bills, $10 bills, $20 bills, and $50 bills to solve this problem.

Kana has four different kinds of bills. She has three times as many of her highest bill as she does her lowest bill. She has twice as many of her second highest bill as her highest bill. She has one more of her second lowest bill than her lowest bill. If she has $257 what are the bills? How many of each does she have?

Line Graph

Plot the sales data for the School Fundraiser on the graph and make a line graph by connecting the dots.

Week	Sales $
1	$447
2	$912
3	$769
4	$272
5	$589
6	$612
7	$788
8	$872
9	$941
10	$998

Sales

$1000
$950
$900
$850
$800
$750
$700
$650
$600
$550
$500
$450
$400
$350
$300
$250
$200
$150
$100

Weeks   1   2   3   4   5   6   7   8   9   10

Thursday

Show Us The Money!

Trekk and Terra are going shopping. Using the exchange rate provided, help them figure out how much money they're actually spending.

Example:

Trekk buys some snacks, which cost $7.13 in Canadian dollars (CAD). If $1 in U.S. dollars (USD) = $1.15 CAD, how much did he spend in USD?

$$\frac{1}{1.15} = \frac{X}{7.13}$$

$$1.15X = 7.13$$

$$X = \frac{7.13}{1.15}$$

$$X = \$6.20 \text{ USD}$$

1 Trekk bought a "Bienvenue au Canada" mug for his dad's office. If it costs $8.99 in CAD, how much does it cost in USD if $1 USD = $1.21 CAD?

2 Dad bought two point blankets for Trekk and Terra. They cost $440 in CAD. What do they cost in USD if $0.82 USD = $1.00 CAD?

3 Terra bought maple candies for her friend, Susan. If the box costs $14 in CAD, how much would the box cost in USD if $1 USD = $1.18 CAD?

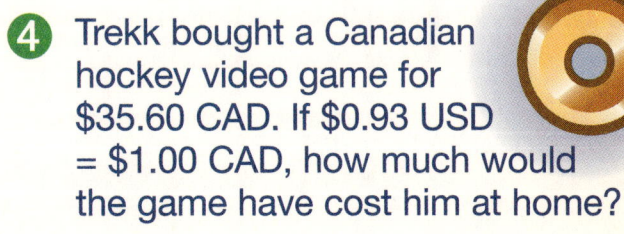

4 Trekk bought a Canadian hockey video game for $35.60 CAD. If $0.93 USD = $1.00 CAD, how much would the game have cost him at home?

5 Terra buys her mother some smoked salmon. She has only $20 USD for this present. If $1 USD = $1.32 CAD, how much can she spend in Canadian dollars?

6 Dad buys a stuffed moose for his wife, for which he pays $14.75 CAD. If $1.00 CAD = $1.17 USD, how much did he spend in U.S. currency?

Crazy Connections!

A *conjunction* is a word that connects parts of a sentence. *Coordinating conjunctions* create a *compound sentence*—a sentence that connects two complete sentences.

Examples:

The cooler itself was destroyed and the water jug was punctured.

Their car didn't have the luxury of the Polar Bear Express, but it seemed more adventurous.

Coordinating Conjunctions

and   but   for   nor   or   so   yet

Turn the 2 columns of sentences into compound sentences by matching them and joining them with coordinating conjunctions.

1. Trekk and Terra were going to take the Polar Bear Express _____

2. The Little Bear had no stops _____

3. During their journey they had much to see _____

4. Trekk and Terra were excited to ride a train _____

5. They took a "water taxi" to the town of Moose Factory _____

6. They boarded the Little Bear to return home _____

A. the train passed by prehistoric beaches and hydroelectric dams.

B. there was no factory that manufactured moose.

C. it stopped whenever someone flagged it down.

D. they discussed their wonderful trip.

E. they wanted to take a "water taxi."

F. they didn't think it would be this cool.

Write a paragraph using only compound sentences. Create at least 3 and use them to tell a story about your favorite adventure.

_____

_____

_____

_____

_____

_____

Friday

Cameras and video cameras are all over the place these days. Describe the last picture or home video you were in, where you were, and why someone felt the need to capture that moment in history.

_____

_____

_____

_____

_____

_____

_____

_____

_____

_____

_____

_____

_____

_____

_____

_____

_____

Un-Bear-able!

A bear, looking for food, broke into Trekk and Terra's cooler. As the kids left the park, they picked up a pamphlet about bear behavior and safety. It had this Bear Math Riddle: What kind of bears do most people meet?

Solve the algebra equations to find out what kind of bear most people meet! The first one is done for you.

1. If there were 136 bear raids over the summer and each bear raided 4 campsites, how many bears were there?

   $4R = 136$ $R = 34$ bears

   $R = \dfrac{136}{4}$

2. There are 55 berry bushes in the park. How many bushes with berries did the bears eat if there are 49 bushes left?

   $55 - H = 49$

3. Nineteen bears were fishing along the river. If they caught 152 fish altogether, how many fish did each bear catch?

   $G \times 19 = 152$

4. The park had 93 bears last year. Twenty-four female bears had cubs. How many cubs did each bear have if the total number of bears has risen to 141?

   $93 + 24U = 141$

5. A curious bear cub watches the northern campground for 28 days and sees 336 people. How many people did it see on average per day?

   $28Y = 336$

6. A female bear needs 10 square km for her territory. If the park is 430 square km, how many female bears can live in the park?

   $10N = 430$

				R	
6	2	43	8	34	12

POSITIVES AND NEGATIVES!

Add the numbers to see if the answers are positive, negative or neutral (0). Then total all the answers to discover whether this whole page is positive, negative or neutral.

1. (+12, -4, +7, -8) = _____

2. (-14, -23, +16, +22) = _____

3. (+26, -19, +14, -21) = _____

4. (+33, -99, +33, +33) = _____

5. (-42, +12, -74, +82) = _____

6. (+16, -17, +14, -21) = _____

7. (+6, -119, +153, -1) = _____

8. (+31, -44, -56, +68) = _____

9. (+123, -79, +64, -121) = _____

10. (-200, -118, +212, +181) = _____

Total Charge for this page (circle one):   POSITIVE   NEGATIVE   NEUTRAL

Pay Dirt!

Matt the Miner must find lodestone—a naturally magnetic ore that resides between 1,200 and 1,400 meters below ground level (or between −1,200 and −1,400). But Matt's a sloppy digger and sometimes doesn't know up from down. Calculate the numbers and use the picture to find where he ends up each day. Each day he starts back at ground level (0).

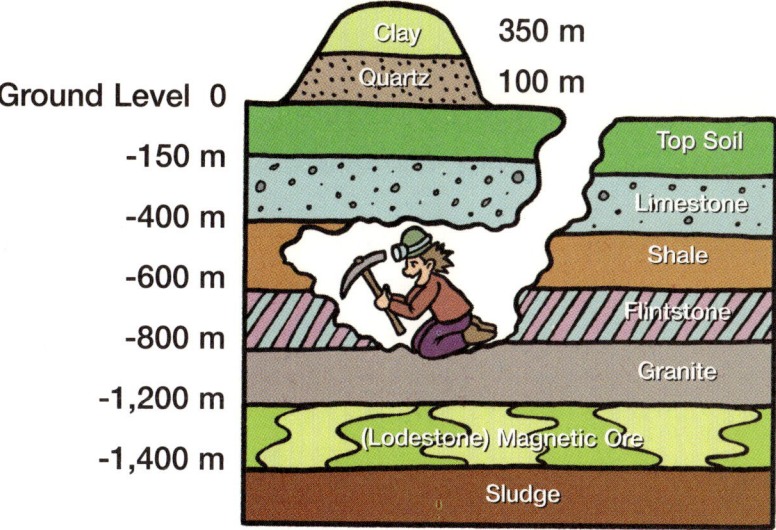

DAY		TOTAL	LOCATION
1.	Down 644, Up 328, Down 747	−1,063	Granite
2.	Down 447, Up 99, Down 212, Up 789		
3.	Down 872, Up 449, Down 887		
4.	Down 338, Up 524, Down 88		
5.	Down 2,049, Up 824, Down 930, Up 210		
6.	Down 1,400, Up 267, Up 693 more, Down 23		
7.	Down 491, Up 712, Down 123, Up 104, Down 29		
8.	Down 94, Up 45, Down 77, Up 29, Down 426, Up 215		
9.	Down 3,429, Up 2,619, Down 3,521, Up 2,262		
10.	Down 5,249, Up 3,839, Down 2,518, Up 2,529		

More Mega Math

Each of the symbols represents a number between 1 - 10. Can you figure out which number should fill in the blank?

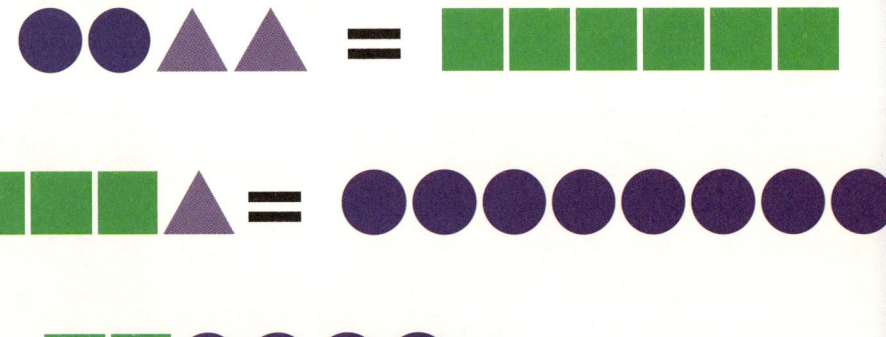

Missing Math!

Fill in the blanks with the numbers 1 - 9 so that the problems make sense. However, you can only use each number one time. The 4 was already put in for you!

$$\underline{\hspace{2cm}}^{(2)} = \underline{\hspace{2cm}}$$

$$\underline{\hspace{2cm}} + \underline{\hspace{2cm}} = \underline{\hspace{2cm}}$$

$$\underline{\hspace{2cm}} \times \underline{\;\;4\;\;} = \underline{\hspace{2cm}}$$

$$\underline{\hspace{2cm}} = \frac{25}{5}$$

Word Problems

Use addition, subtraction, multiplication or division to solve the word problems below.

1 Company X sold 700,000 T-shirts this year. Last year they sold 80% of what they sold this year. What did they sell last year?

2 XYZ Elementary School has 24 teachers and a total of 528 students. What is the average number of students in each class?

3 Happytime Amusement Park has a total of 17 rides. The average wait in line for each is 30 minutes. How many rides could you go on in one 8–hour day if you took one hour for lunch?

4 Barry drinks two gallons of milk each week. How many gallons of milk does he drink in a year?

5 You want to buy a stereo that costs $169.00. You have $76.00 in your bank account and your aunt said she is sending you $40.00 for your birthday. How much money do you still need to buy that stereo?

6 Your baseball team has a record so far of 10 wins to 6 losses. There is a total of 20 games in the season. What is the best possible record your team could finish with this season? What is the worst possible record your team could finish with?

Hudson's Children

CHAPTER TWELVE

As Little Bear moved southward, Trekk's dad told of Henry Hudson's attempts to find a Northeast Passage to China.

"Hudson's idea was to sail to the Pole, turn east, and then work his way down the other side of the world. Ice blocked him twice and winds blew him south, so he found New York Harbor and the Hudson River on the third voyage."

"Pretty far off course," Trekk said.

"That's right. He had heard from Captain John Smith and others that there might be a Northwest Passage across what is now the United States. On his last voyage he discovered Hudson Bay, but ice trapped him in James Bay. Food ran out. Mutiny erupted. Hudson, his young son, and some loyal crewmen were set adrift in a small boat."

"The rest of the crew just left them?" Terra asked.

"No one ever saw or heard from them again, but legend claims that he survived. Marks looking like 'HH' were found. One Inuit story tells of finding a boat with dead men and a live boy. Nobody really knows."

"How sad," Trekk said.

Back in Cochrane, the group began the trip home. They restocked and headed for Sault Ste. Marie.

They took one last afternoon to fish near Chapleau. They watched a loon and tried quietly to approach it with the canoe. Every time they got near, it dove and disappeared. Suddenly, Terra had a terrific strike on her line. She yanked the pole and began to reel when she saw the loon had taken her reel. To her horror, the loon dove under the canoe. "If we don't get him, he'll drown," her uncle said. After some awful moments, a thrashing loon surfaced. Trekk jumped in and put his jacket over the bird. They brought it to shore. Luckily, the hooks had done little damage. Gently, Trekk's dad cut the bird loose and put it in the water. The loon swam weakly away.

"Do you think he'll make it?" Terra asked.

"He has a chance," her uncle replied.

"More than Henry Hudson's young son had," Trekk said, unable to shake the story from his mind.

Terra said, "That's it!"

"What?" Trekk said.

"What if he did make it? What if he survived?"

"Think of all he would have had to go through and learn," Trekk said.

"You two have just solved my problem!" Trekk's dad said. "There's my story!"

"'Hudson's Child,'" said Terra.

"'A Legend of Hope,'" Trekk added.

"That's pretty good. This could turn into a whole book. Can I count on you two for ideas?"

"You bet," the cousins said, laughing.

On fire with ideas, Trekk and Terra promised to work together by e-mail and telephone. Their Ontario trip was ending, but a new adventure was just beginning.

Activity 12

Skill: Summarizing

Put these events and places Terra and Trekk experienced in the right order, beginning with the earliest one. Number the events from 1 to 10.

_____ Hornepayne, after being stuck in the sand

_____ Chapleau and the loon

_____ Entering Canada at Sault Ste. Marie

_____ René Brunelle Provincial Park and the bears

_____ Cochrane and the train station

_____ Lake Superior Provincial Park and the fearsome squirrel

_____ Moosonee and James Bay

_____ Kapuskasing and the moose

_____ Wawa and the giant goose

_____ Back from James Bay aboard Little Bear

Exploring Flight:

The Science of Flight

Introduction to the Project

Humans have long dreamed of soaring high in the air like birds, but for centuries, many believed that if we were meant to fly, we would have wings. That was before the science of aviation took flight. As your child uses hands-on activities to study the basic concepts of aerodynamics, the magic of flight comes alive. Working with objects such as balloons and paper models, your child will learn the physical forces that act upon objects in flight, as well as how those forces can manipulate and control flight patterns.

These enrichment activities require your child to use skills, such as logic and analysis, to learn how to follow directions, make inferences and observations, and draw conclusions. This experience teaches your child how the scientific method is used to test a hypothesis and how the introduction of variables can affect test results. ◆

Master Materials List

8 sheets of 8.5 in. x 11 in. (21.6 cm x 27.9 cm) paper

scissors

2 sheets of colored construction paper

paper clips (at least 30)

masking tape

4 clothespins

4 paper muffin liners

tape measure or yardstick

ruler

pen (blue or black)

box of crayons or nontoxic, washable colored markers

tape (masking tape or invisible tape)

fishing line

2 plastic straws or small sticks

wax paper or plastic wrap

nontoxic glue or paste suitable for paper

pencil

helium balloon

bucket

large plastic self-sealing bag

foam cup

penny

safety pin

(Optional)

nontoxic, washable paints

onion, parchment, or wax paper, cut to 8.5 in. × 11 in. (21.6 cm × 27.9 cm) size

Manila file folder

cereal box

What do you think air is made of? Although air is invisible, it actually has substance, or mass, and weight. Air presses down on the earth all the time. We usually do not notice air pressure unless we fly in the sky, where the pressure is less. Air pushes an airplane forward and helps keep it up in the sky.

Four main forces act on an airplane to make it fly: weight, lift, thrust and drag. In general, weight pulls a plane down, lift pulls a plane up, thrust pushes a plane forward, and drag pulls a plane backward. *See Figure 1.*

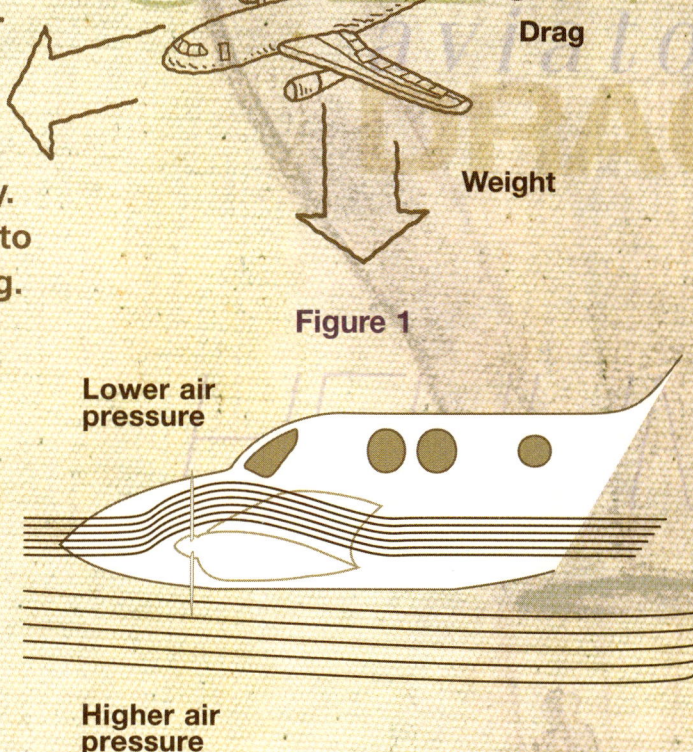

Figure 1

Figure 2

Materials
8.5 in. x 11 in. (21.6 cm x 27.9 cm) paper
scissors

Directions

In the early 1700s, mathematician Daniel Bernoulli discovered that the faster air moves, the lower its pressure is. Because of an airplane wing's teardrop shape, air moves faster over the wing than under it. This causes the air pressure pushing down on the top of the wing to be lower than the pressure pushing up. See *Figure 2.* The difference in pressure causes suction, which pulls the wings up—a process called lift.

1. To see Bernoulli's principle at work, take an 8.5 in. x 11 in. (21.6 cm x 27.9 cm) sheet of paper.

2. Cut the paper in half lengthwise.

3. Hold the short end of one strip of paper to your lips using the forefinger and thumb of both hands as shown. Blow over the top edge of the paper. Watch what happens. See *Figure 3.*

Figure 3

Spinning Maple Seeds

Thrust is the push planes need to move forward. According to Bernoulli's principle, lift is produced when there is a difference in air pressure above and below the wing.

The same theory can be applied to airplane propellers. Air in front of a propeller blade moves faster than air behind it, lowering the air pressure. Lower air pressure in front of a propeller blade thrusts a plane forward, just like lower air pressure above a wing lifts a plane into the air.

Many aviators rely on spinning propellers to give their aircraft the thrust needed to push them through the air. Maple seeds offer scientists a way to study how nature has designed a "perfect propeller" that spins in the air as it floats to the ground. Bernoulli's principle applies to a simple maple seed as well as to the most sophisticated modern aircraft. ◆

Materials

construction paper

scissors

3 paper clips

Directions

Although maple seeds come in a wide variety of shapes and sizes, all of them spin. It is surprisingly difficult to make a model of a maple seed that spins in the same way. See whether you can duplicate nature's "perfect propeller."

1. Cut out the three maple seed templates on the right.

2. Use the templates to trace outlines on construction paper, and cut out construction paper seeds. Label the three seeds "A," "B" and "C."

3. Slightly curl up the edges of each seed as shown.

4. Holding the seeds level, drop them one by one from a height of at least 5 feet (1.5 meters).

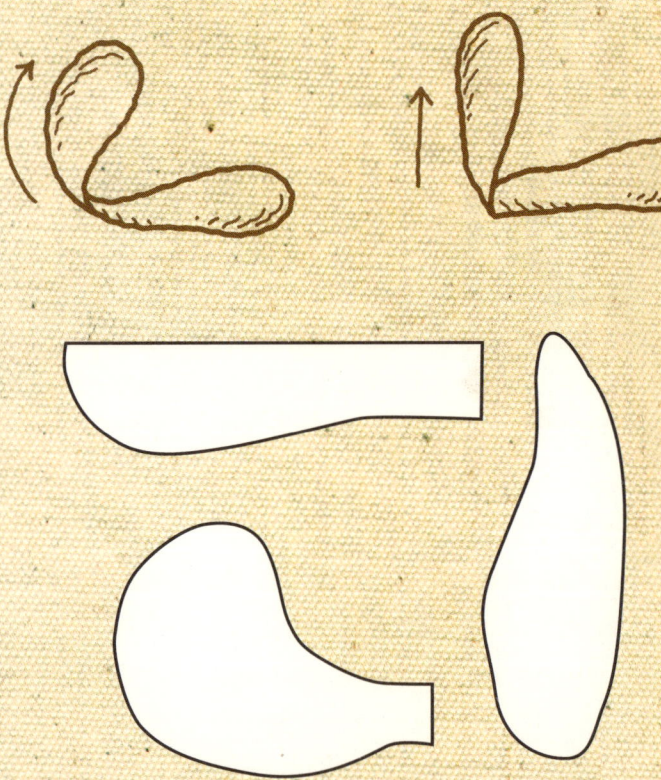

5. If a seed does not spin, experiment with adjusting the shape of the seed. For example, curl the edges of the seed down, or slightly fold the edge of a seed up or down to add a flap.

6. Experiment with creating your own designs of maple seeds.

Super Duper Chopper 'Copter

Drag can slow the movement of an object in flight. Notice how a bird's aerodynamic wings "slice" effortlessly through the air as it glides. Birds are shaped to minimize drag and to counter their weight, as well as the pull of gravity. Gliders and machines that are designed for flight, such as helicopters and airplanes, utilize the design of a bird's wings to reduce drag and help stabilize and control flight. ◆

Materials

scissors
tape
paper clips
Manila file folder
   (optional)
construction paper
   (optional)
cereal box
   (optional)

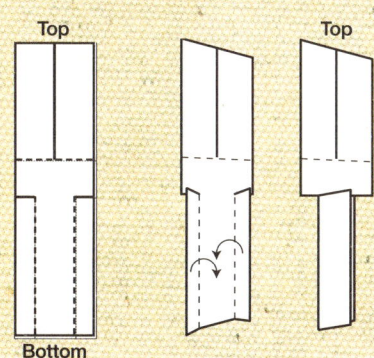

Figure 1   **Figure 2**

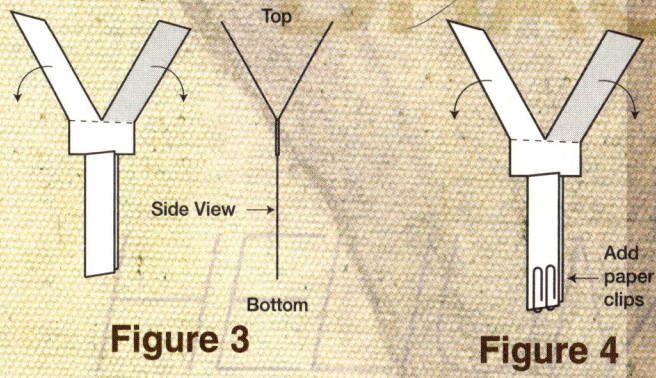

Figure 3   **Figure 4**

Directions

Drag does not just work against pilots when they fly. They can use drag to help control the flight, such as its rate of descent, speed and stability. Create the Super Duper Chopper 'Copter and experiment with the effects of drag and weight.

1. Cut out the rectangle template on the last page of the book. *See Figure 1.*

2. Cut along the short, horizontal, solid lines in the middle of the template. Fold the bottom flaps in along the dotted lines, and tape them to the middle section. *See Figure 2.*

3. Hold the 'copter at a height of approximately 5 ft. (1.5 m) with the bottom pointing down, and drop. Observe how the 'copter flies.

_____

_____

4. Next, cut the vertical line on the top half of the 'copter to create helicopter blades. Bend down the blades to opposite sides along the dotted lines. Keep the blades at a slight angle. *See Figure 3.*

5. Drop the 'copter from the same height. How does it fly this time?

_____

_____

6. Experiment by adding paper clips to the bottom of the 'copter. *See Figure 4.* How does the added weight affect the flight and why?

_____

_____

7. Create 'copters from other materials, such as a Manila file folder, construction paper, or cereal box cardboard. Observe how different materials affect the 'copter's flight.

Exploring Flight:

The Great Glorious Glider Airplane Race

Thrust is what propels an airplane forward through the air. You have seen how propellers can create thrust, but there are many other ways to give an object the boost needed to achieve speed. For example, jet engines provide the great thrust needed to accelerate today's large, heavy aircraft. Solid-rocket boosters and liquid-propellant engines provide the enormous power needed to thrust space shuttles into outer space. ◆

Materials
2 sheets of 8.5 in. × 11 in.
   (21.6 cm × 27.9 cm) paper
pen or pencil

Directions
The same forces that act on real airplanes also apply to paper airplanes. To see how thrust affects the speed and distance of a craft, fold two identical copies of the same paper airplane. Follow these steps to create two Glorious Glider airplanes.

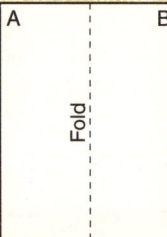

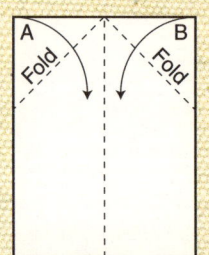

1. Fold the paper in half as shown, and then unfold.

2. Fold the top corners (A and B) to the center fold line. Note: You might want to label the corners as shown as you proceed.

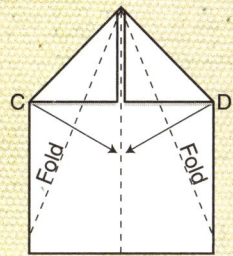

3. Fold the new corners (C and D) to the center fold line.

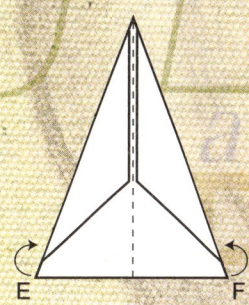

4. Bend the plane backward so that points E and F touch.

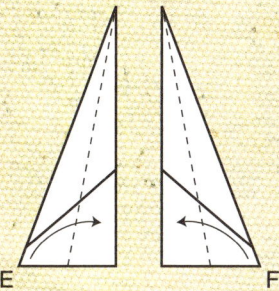

5. To create the wings, fold the plane in half, starting at the point.

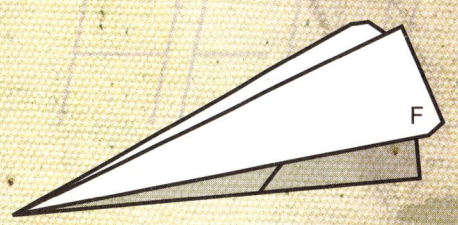

6. Lift up wings E and F.

7. Repeat steps 1 through 6 to make a second plane. Give each plane a name, and mark the name on the top of the plane's wing.

8. Hold one plane in each hand between your thumb and forefinger on the bottom edge at about the midway point. Throw them at the same time in the same direction with equal amounts of force (thrust). Conduct several test flights, using the same hand to throw each plane. Launch the planes using differing amounts of thrust. Does one plane always seem to go faster and/or farther?

9. Switch planes and throw each with the alternate hand. If you are right-handed, does the plane thrown from your right hand usually go faster and/or farther? If you are left-handed, does the plane thrown from your left hand usually go faster and/or farther? Why?

Exploring Flight:

Jet Flier Showdown

For years, engineers and aviators have used flight simulators and models to help refine air travel and improve safety. Researchers closely study how even slight changes to an aircraft's design and materials can influence how it handles and maneuvers in the air. ◆

Materials

1 sheet of 8.5 in. × 11 in.
(21.6 cm × 27.9 cm) paper

construction paper
(or other heavyweight paper)

glue

scissors

onion, parchment, or wax
paper, cut to 8.5 in. × 11 in.
(21.6 cm × 27.9 cm) size
(optional)

tape

Directions

See how the material used to make a Jet Flier can influence how it flies. First, fold two versions of the jet: one using regular-weight copier paper and the other using construction paper or other heavyweight paper. Conduct five test flights for each plane, and record each flight's speed, direction, and distance.

1. As you have done with previous paper planes, fold the paper in half, open it, and fold down the top corners to meet the center fold.

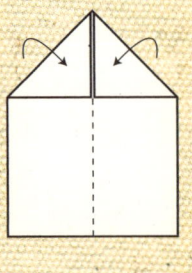

2. Fold the paper in half. The corners should be inside the fold.

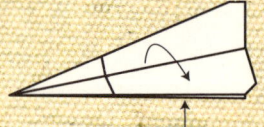

3. Fold down first one side and then the other as shown. Line up the slanted edges to create a pointed nose.

4. Create wings by folding each side again, lining each up with the bottom as shown.

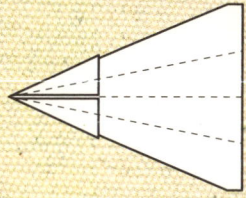

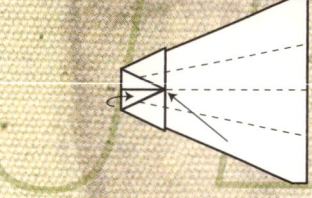

5. Unfold the jet so that it looks like this.

6. Fold the pointed nose tip down so that it meets the overlap. Now the jet has a squared-off nose.

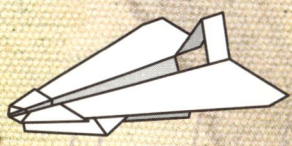

7. Refold the paper in half with the folded nose tip inside. Tape the nose together. Mark a point about 1 in. (2.5 cm) from the back edge of the jet, and cut a vertical line up to the wing fold. This will create a tail.

8. Push the tail you cut in step 7 up through the plane so that it sticks above the plane. Mold it into a triangle shape as shown. Spread the wings slightly.

9. Repeat steps 1-8 using your heavier paper.

10. Experiment by adding more weight to the heavier plane. Spread glue on its wings. Let it dry, and then conduct more flight tests. How does the added weight affect how this jet flies? How might using very light, thin paper affect a jet's flight? See for yourself by folding a Jet Flier, using onion, parchment, or wax paper.

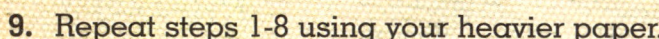

Exploring Flight:

Testing Flight Variables

Changing an aircraft's shape and weight, as well as the places where weight is added or reduced, can make an important difference in how the craft flies. ◆

Materials
paper clips

pencil or pen

scissors

Directions
Choose one of the jets you created on pages 166-167, and conduct a series of tests to measure how certain variables affect its flight. The variables to test include:

• Adding paper clips to the nose and tail of the aircraft

• Adding tail flaps to the aircraft

Use the Jet Flier Data Sheet on the next page to record your estimates of how the variables will affect each flight, as well as the actual results of each fight.

To create wing flaps for Trials 5 and 6, cut two .5 in. (1.3 cm) slits on the rear edge of each wing about 1 in. (2.5 cm) apart. Make the flaps by bending the cut sections up or down.

Jet Flier Data Sheet

Trial Number	Variable Added	Flight Pattern*	Approximate Speed**	Actual Flight Distance***
1	None			
2	Paper clip to nose			
3	Paper clip to tail			
4	Three paper clips to tail			
5	Wing flaps up			
6	Wing flaps down			

*Level, veer left/right, nose dive, tailspin

**Fast, average, slow

***Average of three test flights

Exploring Flight:

Testing Direction with Orville and Wilbur

An experienced pilot can precisely control his or her aircraft's movement and direction. You can control an airplane in flight on three axes: roll, pitch and yaw. Roll occurs when the airplane wings are raised or lowered in opposite directions, causing the plane to rotate from side to side. Pitch results when the nose of the plane goes up or down, causing the entire plane to move up or down. Yaw occurs when the plane's nose aims left or right, causing the plane to turn left or right. ◆

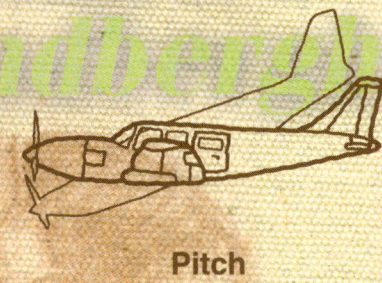

Pitch

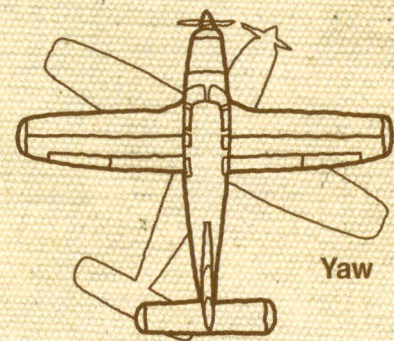

Yaw

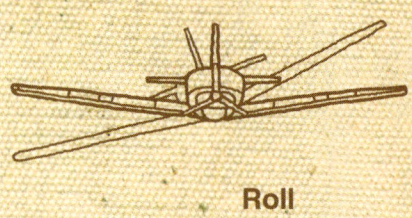

Roll

Materials
pen or pencil
paints, colored markers, or crayons

Directions
Subtle changes made to a paper airplane will impact how the plane flies. Use the non-flap plane you folded on pages 164-165, or fold a new jet. Next, print the name "Orville" clearly on the top of one wing and "Wilbur" on top of the other. See how modifications you make to the jet's wings change its flight path by putting it through a series of test flights. Use the same amount of throw (thrust) for each test. Record your results in the "Charting Directions" form on the next page.

When you have finished with the test, decorate your new jet using markers, paints or crayons.

Charting Directions

Note: For "up" and "down" wing positions, bend the wing up or down at a 45-degree angle from its level (horizontal) position.

45°

Test Flight Number	Wing Position	Flight Direction (level veers left, veers right nose dives, tailspins)	Flight Distance
1	Orville and Wilbur level		
2	Orville up, Wilbur level		
3	Orville and Wilbur up		
4	Wilbur up, Orville level		
5	Orville and Wilbur down		
6	Orville down, Wilbur level		
7	Wilbur down, Orville level		

Which force or forces are acting on the jet to explain the results of your test?

_____

_____

Answers

MONDAY Page 5
Activity 1

Trekk's home is in New York.
Cousin Terra is from New Mexico.
Trekk's dad is a writer.
Terra's mother is an archaeologist.

TUESDAY Page 6
Math Maze

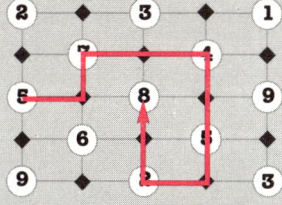

Word Games

1. Nylon. The rest are natural fibers.
2. Dendrite. The rest are teeth.
3. Robin. The others hibernate.

TUESDAY Page 7
Matching

1. f	3. a	5. d	7. h
2. e	4. g	6. c	8. b

WEDNESDAY Page 8
Flip Out!

1. Yes	Both	5. Yes	Bilateral
2. Yes	Rotational	6. No	
3. Yes	Bilateral	7. Yes	Bilateral
4. No		8. No	

WEDNESDAY Page 9
Mega Math

Tom has the following coins:

6 silver dollars	$ 6.00		11 half dollars	$ 5.50
6 half dollars	$ 3.00		11 quarters	$ 2.75
6 dimes	$ 0.60	OR	11 dimes	$ 1.10
6 nickels	$ 0.30		11 nickels	$ 0.55
TOTAL	$ 9.90		TOTAL	$ 9.90

Place Values

1. 60,000,000 + 5,000,000 + 400,000 + 40,000 + 4,000 + 200 + 90 + 9
2. 1,000,000 + 900,000 + 60,000 + 7,000 + 800 + 20 + 2
3. 400,000,000,000 + 70,000,000,000 + 9,000,000,000 + 500,000,000 + 80,000,000 + 6,000,000 + 200,000 + 80,000 + 6,000 + 500 + 30 + 3
4. 800,000,000 + 30,000,000 + 1,000,000 + 400,000 + 80,000 + 1,000 + 900 + 10 + 5

THURSDAY Page 10
Balance the Checking Account

Date	Deposit	Withdrawal	Balance
Jan. 2nd	$208.00		$675.00
Jan. 9th		$88.11	$586.89
Jan. 16th		$256.62	$330.27
Jan. 23rd	$1,211.47		$1,541.74
Jan. 30th		$118.98	$1,422.76
Feb. 6th	$526.50		$1,949.26
Feb. 13th		$733.69	$1,215.57
Feb. 20th	$64.99		$1,280.56
Feb. 27th		$412.53	$868.03
March 6th	$75.75		$943.78
March 13th		$67.88	$875.90
March 20th	$298.98		$1,174.88

THURSDAY Page 11
Capital Events

1. 1607 — Henry Hudson was commissioned by the Muscovoy Company to find a faster way to Asia from England.
2. 1609 — Henry Hudson was given a ship, named Half Moon, by the Dutch East India Company.
3. 1610 — Henry Hudson thought he had entered the Pacific Ocean, but it was actually a very large bay.
4. 1611 — The ship's crew mutinied and cast Hudson and his son adrift in a small boat in what is now Hudson Bay.
5. The bay he entered is now known as Hudson Bay. A strait and a river are also named after him.

WEEK 1 • Continued

FRIDAY Page 13
Trekk's Trekkin'

Nearest Tenth		Nearest Hundredth	
0.7 meters	0.3 meters	0.73 meters	0.29 meters
0.5 meters	1.0 meters	0.49 meters	0.97 meters
0.2 meters	0.4 meters	0.21 meters	0.37 meters
0.9 meters	0.6 meters	0.94 meters	0.56 meters
0.7 meters	0.4 meters	0.66 meters	0.45 meters
Total: 5.7		Total: 5.67	

Total without rounding: 5.661

SATURDAY Page 15
Star Light, Far Light!

1) 11.41	5) 5.97	9) 11.22	13) 8.7	17) 7.8
2) 4.24	6) 11.12	10) 4.34	14) 4.3	18) 10.6
3) 11.25	7) 11.22	11) 11.2	15) 10.4	19) 8.2
4) 8.67	8) 8.55	12) 8.6	16) 11.3	20) 9.5

Parsecs

1) 37.20	5) 19.46	9) 36.58	13) 28.36	17) 25.43
2) 13.82	6) 36.25	10) 14.15	14) 14.02	18) 34.56
3) 36.68	7) 36.58	11) 36.51	15) 33.90	19) 26.73
4) 28.26	8) 27.87	12) 28.04	16) 36.84	20) 30.97

SUNDAY Page 16
More Mega Math

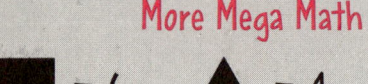

■ = 6   ▲ = 4   ● = 2

Answer: ? = 8
Fractions, Decimals & Percentages

1. $\frac{1}{100}$ = 0.01 = 1%

5. $\frac{98}{100}$ = 0.98 = 98%

2. $\frac{13}{100}$ = 0.13 = 13%

6. $\frac{33}{100}$ = 0.33 = 33%

3. $\frac{66}{100}$ = 0.66 = 66%

7. $\frac{32}{100}$ = 0.32 = 32%

4. $\frac{77}{100}$ = 0.77 = 77%

8. $\frac{42}{100}$ = 0.42 = 42%

SUNDAY Page 17
Similes, Metaphors and Personification

1. a	3. b	5. b	7. c
2. a	4. c	6. a	8. b

WEEK 2 • Pages 18–31

MONDAY Page 19
Activity 2

Answers will vary. Possible responses:

1. Trekk looked taller, and he had changed his hair.
2. Terra is used to flying alone now.
3. They met in Michigan to pick up camping equipment from a friend.
4. They traveled northwest.
5. They saw cherry and apple orchards as they drove through Michigan.
6. They pitch tents and build a campfire. Terra and Trekk take a moonlight hike.
7. The group plans to go sailing the next day.

TUESDAY Page 20
Odd Number Out

1st Row: 63, all others are products of 12. (2x12=24, 6x12=72, 9x12=108, 1x12=12)
2nd Row: 71, all others are products of 11. (3x11=33, 12x11=132, 6x11=66, 1x11=11)
3rd Row: 92, all others are products of 14. (4x14=56, 1x14=14, 2x14=28, 7x14=98)

Adverbial Phrases

1. She ate her hamburger (in a hurry.)
2. He lost his watch (in the back yard.)
3. You better run (as fast as you can.)
4. My uncle works nights and sleeps (during the day.)
5. My brother ran on the treadmill (for an hour.)
6. The mechanic tuned the car (with precision.)

TUESDAY
Matching Page 21

1. e	5. g
2. c	6. d
3. f	7. a
4. h	8. b

WEDNESDAY
Angles Page 22

1. Acute	4. Acute
2. Obtuse	5. Right
3. Right	6. Obtuse

WEDNESDAY Page 23
Mega Math

Potato chips cost $4.70.
Consonants are $0.10 each and vowels are $1.00 each.

Punctuation & Capitalization Quiz

Sara couldn't wait for summer vacation to begin! Her family was planning a trip to Europe. "Mom, when are we leaving for our trip?" asked Sara. "We will leave on June 30," answered Sara's mother.

THURSDAY Page 24
Parts of the Whole System!

1. .2	7. 1	13. .455
2. .75	8. .077	14. .778
3. .7	9. .444	15. .615
4. .375	10. .286	16. .158
5. .4	11. .933	17. .882
6. .583	12. .889	18. .75

THURSDAY Page 25
Canada's Worst Train Disaster

On June 29, 1867, a special passenger train plunged into the Richlieu River near Beloil, killing 97 German immigrants and 2 train conductors. The train headed toward Montreal on the Grand Trunk Railway and went through a drawbridge left open for the passage of barges on the river below. Rescuers from Montreal and local residents worked day and night to recover victims.

Curious crowds gathered at the scene of the accident, contributing to a tense atmosphere. "Imprison the mechanic! It's his fault!" shouted one local woman.

"I know people want answers, but it's too early to make judgments at this time," said one coroner. The investigation will continue over the next few weeks.

FRIDAY Page 27
Comparing Apples To Apples!

1. 3/8	6. 4/5	11. 4/6
2. 1/5	7. 7/8	12. 5/8
3. 4/6	8. 19/21	13. 7/9
4. 1/3	9. 2/11	14. .20
5. 5/8	10. 7/125	15. .8

SATURDAY Page 29
Who's Who in an Ecosystem?

1. 0.6
2. 0.3
3. 0.1
4. 0.4 and 4/10 (or 1/5)
5. 0.9 and 9/10
6. 0.3 consumers, 0.45 producers, and 0.25 decomposers
7. 0.625 consumers, 0.325 producers, and 0.05 decomposers

SUNDAY Page 30
Grid Logic

	Nathan	Tino	Vanessa	Azra	Maple	Oak	Birch	Spruce
Kamali	X	X	X	O	X	O	X	X
Rodriguez	X	X	O	X	X	X	X	O
Bahaligia	X	O	X	X	X	X	O	X
Feinstein	O	X	X	X	O	X	X	X
Maple	O	X	X	X				
Oak	X	X	X	O				
Birch	X	O	X	X				
Spruce	X	X	O	X				

Answer:
1. Nathan Feinstein/Maple
2. Tino Bahaligia/Birch
3. Vanessa Rodriguez/Spruce
4. Azra Kamali/Oak

SUNDAY Page 31
Prefixes

1. disappear
2. misunderstand
3. preview or review
4. reread or misread
5. unsure
6. nonstop

WEEK 3 • Pages 32–45

MONDAY Page 33
Activity 3

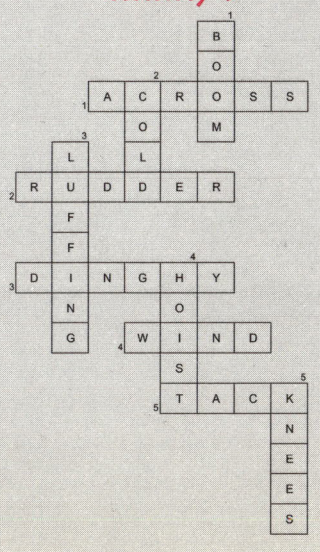

TUESDAY Page 34
Math Maze

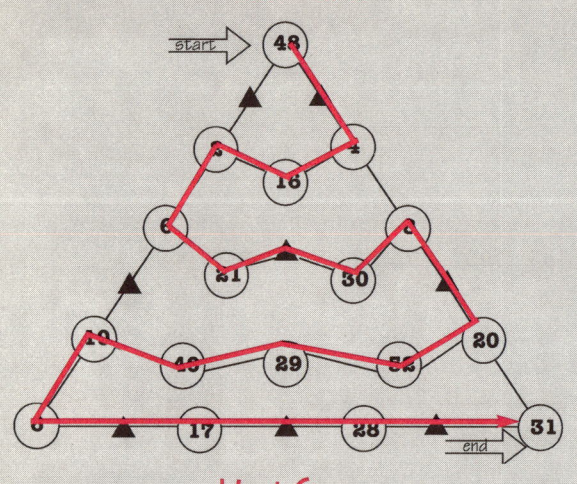

Word Games

1. Carp. The others are saltwater fish.
2. Pig. The others provide milk that can be consumed by humans.
3. Banana. The rest are fruits with pits.

TUESDAY Page 35
Matching

1. d	3. a	5. c	7. h
2. f	4. b	6. g	8. e

WEDNESDAY Page 36
Angle Tangle

1. 45° acute	4. 120° obtuse	7. 115° obtuse	10. 120° obtuse
2. 90° right	5. 90° right	8. 23° acute	11. 40° acute
3. 20° acute	6. 90° right	9. 25° acute	12. 90° right

WEDNESDAY Page 37
Mega Math   Multiplication of Fractions

Jennifer has the following coins:

10 silver dollars	$10.00
10 half dollars	$ 5.00
10 quarters	$ 2.50
10 dimes	$ 1.00
10 nickels	$ .50
TOTAL	$ 19.00

1. e	4. d
2. a	5. c
3. f	6. b

THURSDAY Page 38
Plot the Coordinates

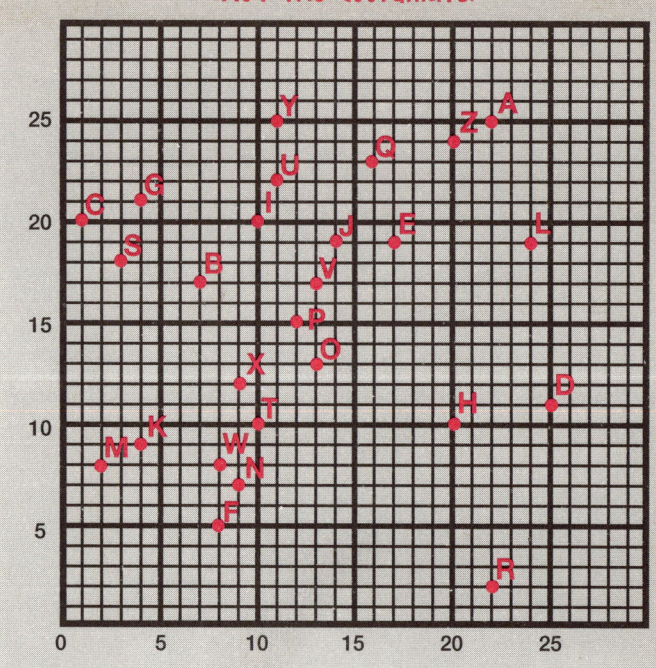

THURSDAY Page 39
Pricey Pronouns

1. his/those ($1.25)	4. answers will vary
2. he/his ($0.75)	5. answers will vary
3. he/himself ($1.25)	6. answers will vary
They have $3.25 for candy.	7. answers will vary

FRIDAY Page 41
Euclid Do It!

1. 2	4. 7	7. 8	10. 11
2. 7	5. 12	8. 1	11. 6
3. 14	6. 4	9. 7	12. 2

SATURDAY Page 42
Forest Life

1. g	4. e	7. f	10. d
2. b	5. k	8. c	11. l
3. h	6. a	9. j	12. i

SATURDAY Page 43
Counting Moose

Trekk's Moose Count

	M	T	W	R	F	Sa	Su	Total	D. Avg
Wk 1	2	2	3	4	1	4	5	21	3
Wk 2	2	2	2	2	2	3	1	14	2
Wk 3	4	0	2	5	3	5	2	21	3
Wk 4	0	0	1	3	4	4	2	14	2
Avg.	2	1	2	3.5	2.5	4	2.5		

Terra's Moose Count

	M	T	W	R	F	Sa	Su	Total	D. Avg
Wk 1	1	2	4	0	2	2	3	14	2
Wk 2	2	3	0	2	1	2	4	14	2
Wk 3	3	1	4	2	5	4	2	21	3
Wk 4	0	0	4	3	7	2	5	21	3
Avg.	1.5	1.5	3	1.5	4	3	3		

Trekk's Dad's Moose Count

	M	T	W	R	F	Sa	Su	Total	D. Avg
Wk 1	4	2	1	4	2	1	0	14	2
Wk 2	2	2	2	4	3	4	4	21	3
Wk 3	1	1	1	0	1	1	2	7	1
Wk 4	5	3	2	4	6	6	2	28	4
Avg.	3	2	1.5	3	3	3	2		

SUNDAY Page 44
More Mega Math

 = 2    = 3    = 1

Answer: ? = 5

Suffixes

1. agreement   3. believable   5. kindly
2. hopeless   4. happiness   6. appearance

SUNDAY Page 45
Calculating Discount Percentages

1. d   3. e   5. f
2. a   4. b   6. c

MONDAY Page 47
Activity 4

1. b   2. c   3. d   4. a   5. d   6. c

TUESDAY Page 48
Odd Number Out

1st Row: 20. (6x6=36, 4x4=16, 3x3=9, 8x8=64)
2nd Row: 42. (5x5=25, 2x2=4, 7x7=49, 6x6=36)
3rd Row: 56. (1x1=1, 4x4=16, 8x8=64, 9x9=81)

All others are perfect squares.

Comparative and Superlative

1. large   larger   largest
2. high   higher   highest
3. big   bigger   biggest
4. quick   quicker   quickest
5. long   longer   longest
6. fast   faster   fastest

TUESDAY Page 49
Matching

1. c   3. e   5. f   7. b
2. d   4. g   6. h   8. a

WEDNESDAY Page 50
Finding Area

1. 150 cm   3. 102 m   5. 2236.5 ft
2. 75 in   4. 344.52 mm   6. 24.2 km

WEDNESDAY Page 51
Mega Math

Favors cost $3.50.
Consonants are $0.50 each and vowels are $0.75 each.

Find the Percent of Each Number

1. .05 x 25 = 1.25   5. .52 x 91 = 47.32
2. .16 x 26 = 4.16   6. .33 x 99 = 32.67
3. .72 x 105 = 75.6   7. .89 x 246 = 218.94
4. .11 x 5 = 0.55   8. .20 x 10 = 2

THURSDAY Page 52
Tourist Trap!

1. $16.87
2. $14.57
3. $3.79
4. $5.77
5. $9.67
6. $6.63

FRIDAY Page 55
"Their Fair Share of Fare!"

1. $\frac{1}{2}$ and $\frac{1}{2}$ Yes
2. $\frac{1}{3}$ and $\frac{1}{5}$ No
3. $\frac{3}{10}$ and $\frac{3}{10}$ Yes
4. $\frac{9}{10}$ and $\frac{9}{10}$ Yes
5. $\frac{4}{11}$ and $\frac{5}{11}$ No
6. $\frac{9}{11}$ and $\frac{12}{19}$ No
7. $\frac{17}{19}$ and $\frac{17}{19}$ Yes
8. $\frac{9}{11}$ and $\frac{9}{11}$ Yes
9. $\frac{4}{21}$ and $\frac{5}{12}$ No
10. $\frac{3}{8}$ and $\frac{5}{6}$ No
11. $\frac{1}{2}$ and $\frac{1}{2}$ Yes
12. $\frac{7}{9}$ and $\frac{7}{9}$ Yes
13. $\frac{9}{11}$ and $\frac{7}{8}$ No
14. $\frac{53}{81}$ and $\frac{7}{12}$ No
15. $\frac{1}{3}$ and $\frac{1}{3}$ Yes

SATURDAY Page 56
Busy Glaciers

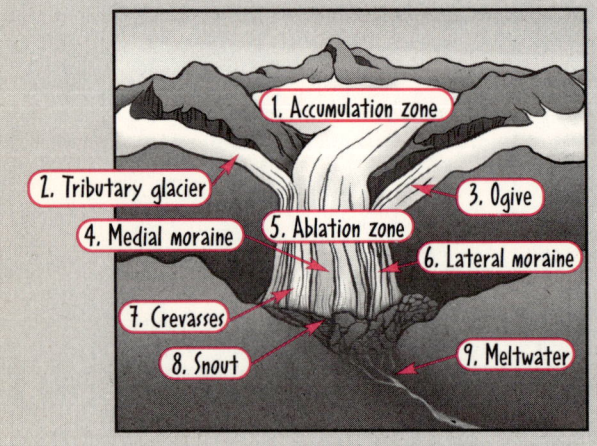

1. Accumulation zone
2. Tributary glacier
3. Ogive
4. Medial moraine
5. Ablation zone
6. Lateral moraine
7. Crevasses
8. Snout
9. Meltwater

SATURDAY Page 57
Swans In Flight

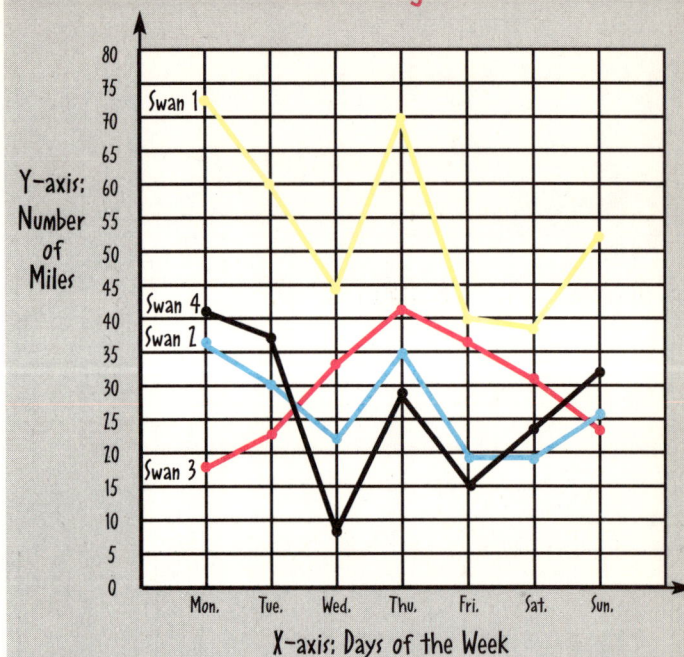

Answer: Swan 1=54, Swan 2=27, Swan 3=29.71, Swan 4=26.71

SUNDAY Page 58
More Mega Math

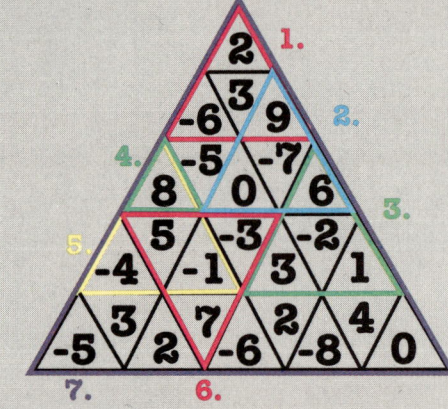

1. $2 + 3 - 6 + 9 = 8$
2. $9 - 7 + 0 + 6 = 8$
3. $6 - 2 + 3 + 1 = 8$
4. $8 = 8$
5. $8 + 5 - 4 - 1 = 8$
6. $5 - 3 - 1 + 7 = 8$
7. The entire triangle adds up to 8.

Brain Teaser

Answer: Shoe. All the others are types of cakes.

SUNDAY Page 59
Fill in the Homonyms

1. I have an eyelash in my eye.
2. My mother needs to go by the bakery to buy a cake.
3. Did you know that there are no more tickets available?
4. My father's sister, Aunt Sara, has an ant farm.
5. Where did you find the Halloween costume you plan to wear?
6. Sam's dad said, "Son, put on some sunblock. That sun is really strong."
7. Did you hear the teacher tell us to come over here?
8. I read the book with the red cover.
9. I want to eat two cookies, too.
10. Let's meet at the market and buy the meat for the cookout.

MONDAY Page 61
Activity 5

1. Detroit
2. White Cloud
3. Petoskey
4. Mackinaw City
5. Whitefish Point
6. Sault Ste. Marie
7. Lake Superior Provincial Park

TUESDAY Page 62
Math Maze

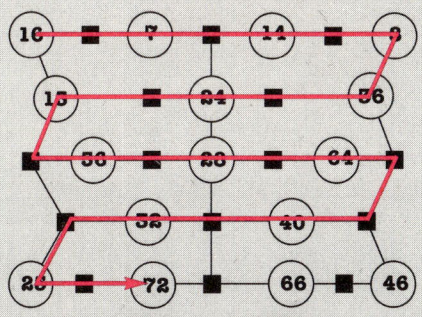

The number is 333.

Word Games

1st Row: They are all things that float.

2nd Row: They are all things that sting.

3rd Row: They are all first names of U.S. presidents.
(John F. Kennedy, Abraham Lincoln, George Washington, Ronald Reagan)

TUESDAY Page 63
Matching

1. c
2. h
3. g
4. f
5. d
6. a
7. b
8. e

WEDNESDAY Page 64
Get Back On Track!

Pile #1: 36 square meters

Pile #2: 45 square meters

Pile #3: 18 square meters

Pile #4: 24 square meters

Pile #5: 15 square meters

No, they'll only need piles 1–4 to get back to the road.

The total is 138 square meters.

There will be 23 square meters left over.

WEDNESDAY Page 65
Mega Math

Holly has the following coins:

42 silver dollars	$42.00
42 quarters	$10.50
42 nickels	$ 2.10
42 pennies	$ 0.42
TOTAL	$55.02

Comparative and Superlative

Word	Comparative	Superlative
1. horrible	more horrible	most horrible
2. generous	more generous	most generous
3. terrific	more terrific	most terrific
4. delicious	more delicious	most delicious
5. ridiculous	more ridiculous	most ridiculous
6. complicated	more complicated	most complicated

THURSDAY Page 66
Pie Graphs

City Name	Percent	Decimal	Population
City A	32%	.32	160,160
City B	28%	.28	140,140
City C	22%	.22	110,110
City D	11%	.11	55,055
City E	3%	.03	15,015
City F	4%	.04	20,020

THURSDAY Page 67
Mad Inventors!

Answers will vary, but here are some possible responses:

1. Louis-Jacques-Mandé Daguerre, the developer of the first photograph in 1826–1827, was born near Paris, France.

2. In 1924, John Larson created the polygraph test, known as a lie detector test.

3. DVDs, invented in 1995, have better quality pictures than videocassettes.

4. James Naismith, the creator of the game of basketball, was a physical education teacher.

5. Cell phones, invented in 1988, allow people to call friends from anywhere.

WEEK 5 •

FRIDAY Page 69 "Percent Advantage!"

1. 50%   3. 25%   5. 67%
2. 20%   4. 10%   6. 75%

SATURDAY Page 70
The Long Way Home

WEEK 1: Mean **416.7**   WEEK 3: Mean **12,285.7**   WEEK 5: Mean **1,975**
         Mode **250**   Mode **13,000**   Mode **400**

WEEK 2: Mean **3,528.6**   WEEK 4: Mean **10,000**
         Mode **1,200**   Mode **10,000**

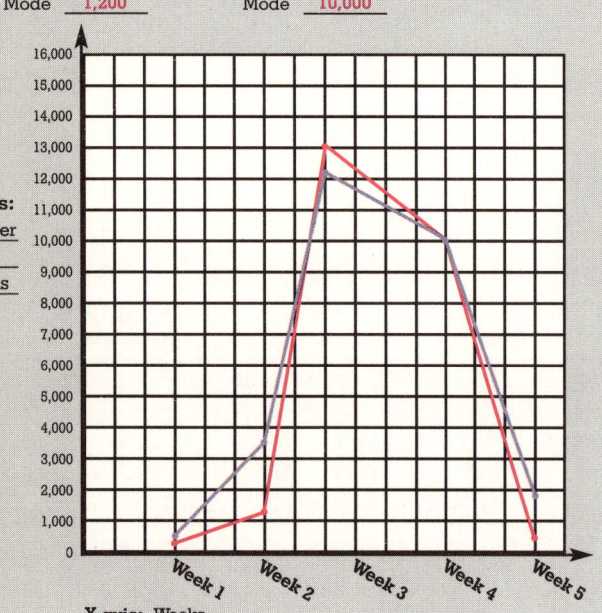

Y-axis: Number of Swans

X-axis: Weeks

SATURDAY Page 71
It's for the Birds!

Canadian Geese		
Captured	20	100%
U.S. tag	5	25%
Cdn. tag	7	35%
Untagged	8	40%

Cranes		
Captured	16	100%
U.S. tag	4	25%
Cdn. tag	8	50%
Untagged	4	25%

Atlantic Brants		
Captured	20	100%
U.S. tag	5	25%
Cdn. tag	5	25%
Untagged	10	50%

Harlequin Ducks		
Captured	50	100%
U.S. tag	10	20%
Cdn. tag	24	48%
Untagged	16	32%

Whistling Swans		
Captured	40	100%
U.S. tag	6	15%
Cdn. tag	14	35%
Untagged	20	50%

Snow Geese		
Captured	200	100%
U.S. tag	34	17%
Cdn. tag	88	44%
Untagged	78	39%

Common Eiders		
Captured	60	100%
U.S. tag	27	45%
Cdn. tag	15	25%
Untagged	18	30%

Black Ducks		
Captured	90	100%
U.S. tag	36	40%
Cdn. tag	27	30%
Untagged	27	30%

Common Terns		
Captured	500	100%
U.S. tag	120	24%
Cdn. tag	125	25%
Untagged	255	51%

SUNDAY Page 72
More Mega Math

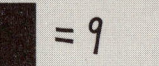 = 9   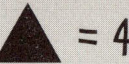 = 4    = 7

Answer: ? = 13

Converting Fractions to Decimals

1. $\frac{17}{1000} = 0.017$ 5. $5\frac{5}{1000} = 5.005$

2. $5\frac{199}{1000} = 5.199$ 6. $792\frac{1777}{10000} = 792.1777$

3. $6\frac{35}{10000} = 6.0035$ 7. $\frac{84}{1000} = 0.084$

4. $\frac{999}{10000} = 0.0999$ 8. $2\frac{27}{10000} = 2.0027$

SUNDAY Page 73
Fantasy vs. Reality

1. Fantasy   5. Reality
2. Reality   6. Fantasy
3. Fantasy   7. Reality
4. Fantasy   8. Fantasy

WEEK 6 • Pages 74–87

MONDAY Page 75
Activity 6

Answers will vary. Possible responses:

1. All the other people were used to the cool temperatures, but Trekk and Terra weren't.
2. The Ojibway are a native people who settled the area long before the French.
3. The Ojibway word Wawa means "Wild Goose" or "Land of Big Goose."
4. The people of the town wanted to attract visitors.
5. They noticed fewer and fewer signs of people.
6. The clearings were built to park construction equipment when the highway was being built.
7. The truck got stuck in the soft sand.
8. The travelers will be behind in their travels. The travelers could experience unexpected adventure.

TUESDAY Page 76
Odd Number Out

1st Row: 35

2nd Row: 18

3rd Row: 88

All the others are prime numbers.
(Their only factors are 1 and themselves.)

Comparative and Superlative Exceptions

1. good   better   best
2. less   lesser   least
3. some   more   most
4. bad   worse   worst

TUESDAY
Page 77
Matching

1. e	3. h	5. a	7. f
2. g	4. b	6. d	8. c

WEDNESDAY Page 78
Sail Away!

1. 16 square feet (1.5 square meters)
2. 17.5 square feet (1.6 square meters)
3. 18 square feet (1.7 square meters)
4. 20 square feet (1.8 square meters)
5. 16.5 square feet (1.7 square meters)
6. 22.5 square feet (2.1 square meters)

They should buy the Blue Thunder sail.

WEDNESDAY Page 79
Mega Math

Paints cost $16.00.
Consonants are $3.00 each and vowels are $2.00 each.

Riddles

1. Snail   2. Fire   3. Mercury

THURSDAY Page 81
Vital Verbs

(Answers can differ from the one provided)

He received word from his family that he would be moving to western Canada. The Canadian government offered free land to people who moved to the prairies. There was no time for anything but packing and preparing for the trip. They did not have the money to buy a wagon, so they traveled west on an ox cart that his father built. He made the cart completely out of wood. Instead of using iron to hold the frames, he used wooden pegs. His friends might have thought waiting was tiresome, but he was always out exploring. He watched the traders trade for furs and game meat. He watched laborers build the railway, which went from the Atlantic to the Pacific. The journey to the prairies was difficult, but it was fun to see so many new things.

FRIDAY Page 83
Ratio Riddles!

1. 2:7; 2:7   3. 1:6   5. 3:11   7. 2:7

2. 4:1; 4:1   4. 1:3; 1:3   6. 5:3

8. A ratio can tell you in very simple numbers, like 1:3, what happens with very LARGE numbers. For instance, the ratio of weekend days to weekdays is 2 out of 7, even if you're covering a whole year, or ten years, or 1500 years! The ratio of breakfasts to all your other meals is 1:3 for one day, ten days, ten years, or 1500 years... if you should live so long. So ratios help you understand very large numbers.

SATURDAY Page 84
Current Events!

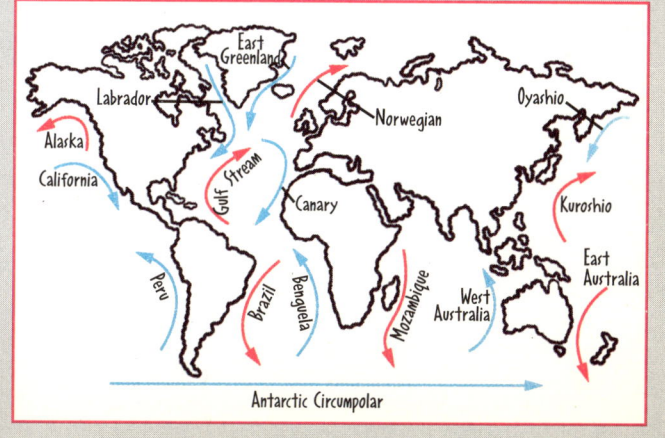

SATURDAY Page 85
What's the Solution?

1. 50	3. 2:5	5. 546
2. 140	4. 350	6. 125

SUNDAY Page 86
More Mega Math

0	-3	5	-4	1	-5
6	2	1	0	-2	8
2	-3	4	3	7	-9
-1	0	-2	0	1	10
1	5	-8	-9	-6	0
2	2	6	-2	7	4

1. 6 + 2 − 3 + 0 = 5
2. 5 − 3 + 2 + 1 = 5
3. 5 = 5
4. 5 + 2 + 1 + 0 + 4 + 3 − 3 − 4 − 3 = 5
5. 10 + 1 − 6 + 0 = 5
6. 7 + 4 + 0 − 6 = 5
7. 0 + 1 + 9 + 6 + 7 − 2 − 8 − 6 − 2 = 5
8. 6 − 2 + 9 − 8 = 5
9. 5 + 2 + 6 − 8 = 5
10. 5 = 5
11. 2 + 2 + 6 − 8 + 5 + 1 − 1 + 0 − 2 = 5
12. 1 + 5 + 0 − 1 = 5
13. 4 + 3 + 0 − 2 = 5
14. 2 + 1 + 0 + 3 + 4 − 3 + 0 − 2 + 0 = 5

Word Pictures

1. split personality
2. lost in space
3. read between the lines
4. time in a bottle
5. strawberry shortcake
6. day after tomorrow
7. live and learn
8. light at the end of the tunnel

WEEK 7 • Pages 88–101

MONDAY Page 89
Activity 7

Answers will vary. Possible responses:
1. I might have taken a cell phone along to call for help.
2. Yes. The story has talked about bear and moose before this.

Answers continued next column

MONDAY Page 89 – Continued

3. No. The situation is not much different from being in a campground.
4. Yes. I would have gotten bored and I would have wanted to help.
5. Getting under the truck is dangerous. They might be running out of supplies.
6. I think Trekk's dad will think of a way to get the truck loose.

TUESDAY Page 90
Math Maze

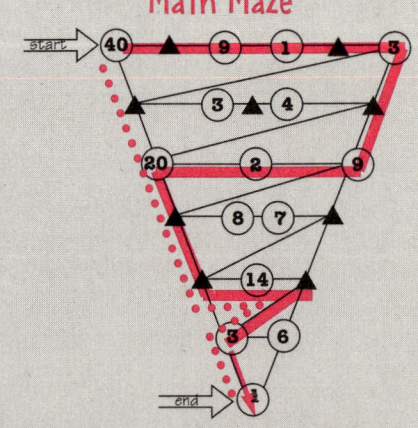

No Double Negatives

1. She didn't say anything.
2. There weren't any shoes left in my size.
3. He doesn't know anybody in his new school.
4. Don't leave any of the milk in your glass.

TUESDAY Page 91
Matching

1. e	3. d	5. f	7. b
2. h	4. g	6. c	8. a

WEDNESDAY Page 92
Finding Radius, Diameter and Circumference

	Circumference	Diameter	Radius
1.	6 ft	2 ft	1 ft
2.	42 cm	14 cm	7 cm
3.	36 m	12 m	6 m
4.	24 mm	8 mm	4 mm
5.	4,872 cm	1,624 cm	812 cm
6.	75 mi	25 mi	12.5 mi
7.	933 in	311 in	155.5 in
8.	307.2 yd	102.4 yd	51.2 yd
9.	2.64 km	.88 km	.44 km
10.	1,263 ft	421 ft	210.5 ft
11.	22,836 cm	7,612 cm	3,806 cm
12.	.69 mm	.23 mm	.115 mm
13.	573 m	191 m	95.5 m
14.	2.997 cm	.999 cm	0.4995 cm

WEDNESDAY   Page 93
Mega Math

The football team has these coins:

12 silver dollars	$12.00	12 nickels	$ 0.60
12 half dollars	$ 6.00	12 pennies	$ 0.12
12 quarters	$ 3.00	TOTAL	$22.92
12 dimes	$ 1.20		

Ratio Quiz

1. c   3. a   5. b
2. f   4. e   6. d

THURSDAY   Page 94
Place Value with Decimals

	Hundreds	Tens	Ones	And	Tenths	Hundredths	Thousandths
1.	6	4	9	•	6	9	2
2.		5	1	•	0	0	5
3.	7	3	3	•	3	4	
4.	4	8	4	•	5	1	1
5.	8	0	1	•	2		
6.	5	6	6	•	7	1	3

THURSDAY   Page 95
Can Do Spirit!

The Cree <u>are</u> the largest native group in Canada. Their tribe <u>had</u> begun in the woodlands around the James Bay. As their population grew they began to spread out across Canada. Groups <u>were</u> spreading out throughout Canada to collect more pelts to trade with the European trading posts that <u>had</u> been established. They <u>were</u> able to gain many things from the Europeans such as new technology. They also acquired horses from them and many tribes moved and settled in the plains. Despite disease and warfare, the Cree <u>were</u> able to survive. Today there <u>are</u> tribal members that live in reservations in the United States while others <u>have</u> been living in the many provinces of Canada. The ancestral language <u>is</u> still spoken by many of the elders today.

FRIDAY   Page 97
Easy "Times"

50 x 7 = 350	40 x 500 = 20,000
40 x 8 = 320	60 x 700 = 42,000
3 x 90 = 270	200 x 50 = 10,000
20 x 20 = 400	400 x 80 = 32,000
80 x 70 = 5,600	30 x 300 = 9,000
60 x 60 = 3,600	200 x 60 = 12,000
5 x 50 = 250	900 x 60 = 54,000
8 x 90 = 720	50 x 700 = 35,000
60 x 1 = 60	800 x 30 = 24,000
40 x 90 = 3,600	500 x 60 = 30,000
80 x 10 = 800	80 x 800 = 64,000
60 x 50 = 3,000	90 x 400 = 36,000

SATURDAY   Page 98
Will Polar Bears Go With the Floe?

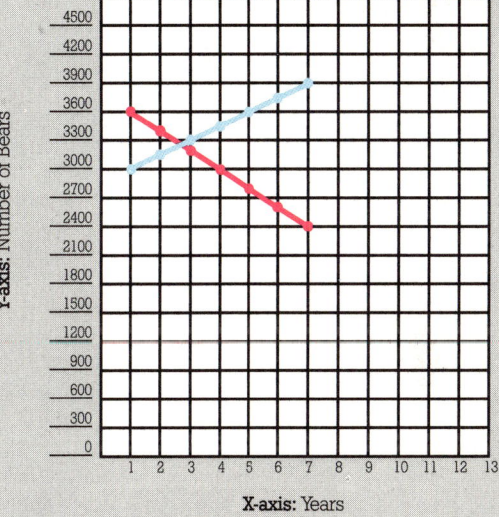

Y-axis: Number of Bears
X-axis: Years

There will be 1,800 Southern Bears in Year 10.

There will be 800 Southern Bears in Year 15.

In Year 19, there should be no more Southern Bears left.

There will be 4,950 Northern Bears in Year 14.

There will be 6,000 Northern Bears in Year 21.

It's very unlikely that Northern Bears will become extinct.

SATURDAY   Page 99
It'll Probably Happen!

1. 1:3   4. 2:6 (or 1:3)   7. 3:3 (or 1:1)   10. 4:6 (or 2:3)   13. 1:3   16. 2:6 (or 1:3)
2. 2:3   5. 3:8   8. 2:3   11. 6:6 (or 1:1)   14. 1:3   17. 2:8 (or 1:4)
3. 1:6   6. 5:8   9. 3:6 (or 1:2)   12. 3:8   15. 1:6   18. 2:8 (or 1:4)

SUNDAY   Page 100
More Mega Math

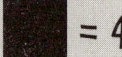 = 4   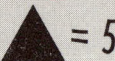 = 5    = 3

Answer: ? = 8

Number Puzzle Box

8	3	4
1	5	9
6	7	2

SUNDAY   Page 101
Subject and Predicate

1. My math book (is so heavy.)
2. The macaroni and cheese (tastes salty.)
3. Sara (fell on the playground.)
4. Bill (learned to water ski last summer.)
5. Mimi's sunglasses (are purple with silver sequins.)
6. I (baked a chocolate cake today.)
7. My dad's car (is being repaired.)
8. The towel (is still wet.)
9. I (have sand between my toes.)
10. Harold (played with his nephews.)

WEEK 8 • Pages 102–115

MONDAY   Page 103
Crossword

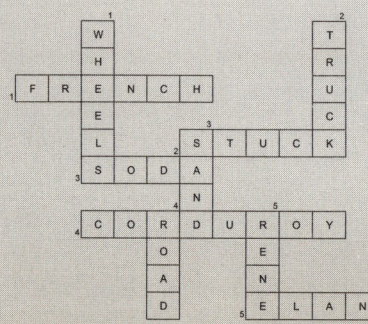

TUESDAY   Page 104
Odd Number Out

1st row:
82. All others are products of 9.
(9x1=9, 9x14=126, 9x5=45, 9x3=27)

2nd row:
12. All others are products of 8.
(8x1=8, 8x12=96, 8x6=48, 8x9=72)
OR
8. All others are products of 12.
(12x8=96, 12x4=48, 12x1=12, 12x6=72)

3rd row:
15. All others are products of 6.
(6x12=72, 6x6=36, 6x1=6, 6x9=54)

Word Pictures

A. Hopscotch
B. Condensed milk
C. Water under the bridge
D. Banana split
E. Walking on water
F. Green with envy
G. Surround sound
H. Play by play

TUESDAY   Page 105
Matching

1. c	3. g	5. h	7. a
2. e	4. b	6. d	8. f

WEDNESDAY   Page 106
Perfect Circles!

1. Diameter 12   Circumference 37.68
2. Diameter 7   Circumference 21.98
3. Diameter 8   Circumference 25.12
4. Diameter 24   Circumference 75.36
5. Diameter 4.4 Circumference 13.82
6. Diameter 17.6 Circumference 55.26

The lake has a diameter of one and a half miles.
The circumference is 4.71 miles.

WEDNESDAY   Page 107
Mega Math

The sleeping bag costs $28.00. Multiply the number of consonants by the number of vowels.

Riddles

1. Maryland   2. A river   3. Ohio   4. The letter "E"

THURSDAY   Page 108
Estimation

1.	100 × 900 = 90,000	3.	100 × 100 = 10,000	5.	600 × 700 = 420,000	7.	400 × 400 = 160,000
2.	500 × 500 = 250,000	4.	600 × 900 = 540,000	6.	300 × 200 = 60,000	8.	800 × 800 = 640,000

THURSDAY Page 109
Setting the Scene

One day, Manobozho went out looking for his cousin, but couldn't find him anywhere.

Instead, he saw the trail of a huge snake and he knew that Meshekenabek, the monster snake whose eyes glowed with fire and scales glistened, had kidnapped his cousin. So he followed the trail to the shore of Manitou Lake, where Meshekenabek lived at the bottom all coiled up in a thicket of hissing snakes.

Angry and swearing revenge for his cousin, Manobozho asked the sun to beat down fiercely on the lake. He wanted the lake to get so hot that Meshekenabek would have to crawl out into the shade of the trees along the shore. Manobozho snuck into these trees and hid himself in a tree stump.

The sun heated Manitou Lake until it was boiling hot. Soon, bubbles started coming to the surface. That's when Meshekenabek lifted his head above the water, looking for Manobozho. He saw the tree stump and said, "Aha! Manobozho has disguised himself!"

Hot waves dashed against the rocks as he and the other snakes slithered and slunk toward the shore and the tree stump. One of the snakes wound his tail around the stump and tried to pull it down, but Manobozho held on.

When Meshekenabek crept into the shade to cool down, Manobozho came out of his disguise and shot an arrow at him. Meshekenabek howled with anger! The snakes began to attack Manobozho! The waters of Manitou Lake began to rise so that the whole world began to flood!

Manobozho warned all the people and animals to run. He and all the people and all the animals took refuge on a mountaintop. But the flood continued to rise, so Manobozho built a great raft for all of them. Eventually the water covered the mountaintop, and Manobozho and all the people and all the animals floated for many days.

FRIDAY Page 111
The Simple Power of Exponents!

1. $5^1 = 25$
2. $8^2 = 64$
3. $10^1 = 100$
4. $12^2 = 144$
5. $36^1 = 1,296$
6. $3^3 = 27$
7. $10^3 = 1,000$
8. $8^3 = 512$
9. $15^3 = 3,375$
10. $7^4 = 2,401$
11. $10^4 = 10,000$
12. $2^5 = 32$
13. $7 \times 7 = 49$
14. $11 \times 11 = 121$
15. $16 \times 16 = 256$
16. $(8 \times 8) \times 8 = 512$
17. $(13 \times 13) \times 13 = 2,197$
18. $(3 \times 3) \times (3 \times 3) = 81$

SATURDAY Page 112
Speedy Exponents

1. 32
2. 1,000
3. 27
4. 10,000
5. 256
6. 243
7. 1,000,000
8. 81
9. 100,000
10. 4,096
11. 10,064
12. 17
13. 513
14. 187

SATURDAY Page 113   Metric Road Trip!

	Kilometers	Meters	Decimeters	Centimeters	Millimeters
Detroit to Petoskey	362	362×10^3	362×10^4	362×10^5	362×10^6
		362,000	3,620,000	36,200,000	362,000,000
Petoskey to Moosonee	708	708×10^3	708×10^4	708×10^5	708×10^6
		708,000	7,080,000	70,800,000	708,000,000
New York to Detroit	837	837×10^3	837×10^4	837×10^5	837×10^6
		837,000	8,370,000	83,700,000	837,000,000
New York to Los Angeles	4,828	$4,828 \times 10^3$	$4,828 \times 10^4$	$4,828 \times 10^5$	$4,828 \times 10^6$
		4,828,000	48,280,000	482,800,000	4,828,000,000
Halifax to Vancouver	5,552	$5,552 \times 10^3$	$5,552 \times 10^4$	$5,552 \times 10^5$	$5,552 \times 10^6$
		5,552,000	55,520,000	555,200,000	5,552,000,000

SUNDAY Page 114
More Mega Math

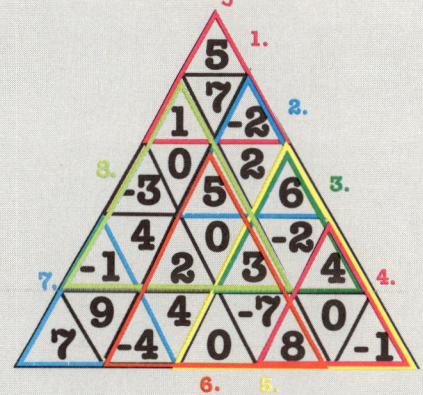

1. $5 + 7 + 1 - 2 = 11$
2. $-2 + 2 + 5 + 6 = 11$
3. $6 - 2 + 3 + 4 = 11$
4. $4 + 0 + 8 - 1 = 11$
5. $6 + 3 - 2 + 4 + 0 - 7 + 8 + 0 - 1 = 11$
6. $5 + 0 + 2 + 3 + 4 - 4 + 0 - 7 + 8 = 11$
7. $-1 + 9 + 7 - 4 = 11$
8. $1 + 0 - 3 + 5 + 4 - 1 + 2 + 0 + 3 = 11$

Brain Teaser

Answer: EAT. The others are names of months with the first letter removed. (jUNE, mAY, mARCH, jULY)

SUNDAY Page 115   Division of Fractions

1. $\frac{1}{2}$
2. $1\frac{11}{45}$
3. $\frac{3}{5}$
4. $1\frac{13}{15}$
5. $2\frac{4}{5}$
6. $1\frac{3}{4}$
7. 9
8. $\frac{5}{6}$

MONDAY Page 117
Activity 9

1. d   2. b   3. b   4. b   5. c

TUESDAY Page 118
Grid Logic

	Dawn	Lucas	Estaban	Michael	Emma	Metalheads	Stonestown Symphony	Wild Yahoos	Backyard Blues Band	Country Kickin'	Monday	Wednesday	Thursday	Friday	Saturday
Montgomery	O	X	X	X	X	X	X	O	X	X	X	O	X	O	X
Hawthorne	X	X	X	X	O	X	X	O	X	X	X	X	X	X	O
Guerro	X	X	O	X	X	X	X	X	X	O	O	X	O	X	X
Juarez	X	X	X	O	X	X	X	X	O	X	X	X	O	X	X
Chen	X	O	X	X	X	O	X	X	X	X	X	X	X	X	O
Monday	X	X	O	X	X	X	X	X	X	O					
Wednesday	O	X	X	X	X	X	X	O	X						
Thursday	X	X	X	X	O	X	X	X	O						
Friday	X	O	X	X	X	O	X	X	X						
Saturday	X	X	X	X	O	X	O	X	X						
Metalheads	X	O	X	X	X										
Stonestown Symphony	X	X	X	X	O										
Wild Yahoos	O	X	X	X	X										
Backyard Blues Band	X	X	X	O	X										
Country Kickin'	X	X	O	X	X										

Answer:
1. Dawn Montgomery/Wild Yahoos/Wednesday
2. Lucas Chen/Metalheads/Friday
3. Estaban Guerro/Country Kickin'/Monday
4. Michael Juarez/Backyard Blues Band/Thursday
5. Emma Hawthorne/Stonestown Symphony/Saturday

TUESDAY Page 119
Matching

1. f   3. e   5. d   7. b
2. h   4. c   6. a   8. g

WEDNESDAY Page 120
Skate Monster 360s!

1. Radius = 49", diameter = 98", circumference = 307.7", angle = 308°
2. Radius = 105 cm, diameter = 210 cm, circumference = 659.4 cm, angle = 323°
3. Radius = 43", diameter = 86", circumference = 270", angle = 264°
4. Radius = 98 cm, diameter = 196 cm, circumference = 615.4 cm, angle = 253°
5. Radius = 41 cm, diameter = 82 cm, circumference = 257.5 cm, angle = 319°

WEDNESDAY Page 121
Mega Math

James has these bills:

4 fifties	$200.00
4 twenties	$ 80.00
4 tens	$ 40.00
4 fives	$ 20.00
TOTAL	$340.00

Riddle

1. The Moon   2. A hole

THURSDAY Page 122
Read the Graph

1. November   2. February   3. 227   4. 380.92

THURSDAY Page 123   Don't Be Negative!

My husband is a voyageur working for the Hudson's Bay Company. I hardly have no (hardly have any) time to spend with him because there always isn't no time (isn't any). He is so busy establishing posts along the James Bay and Hudson Bay. My husband don't catch no (doesn't catch any) animals. Members of other tribes bring in the furs and trade them for goods. The tribes need items made of metal like knives and weapons since they don't have no (don't have any) way of making it themselves. This sure ain't no (isn't a) good way to work. They ain't going to be no (aren't going to be any) help to themselves. There just isn't no (isn't any) good that will come of it.

FRIDAY Page 125
Please Excuse My Dear Aunt Sally!

1. 22   3. 13   5. 156   7. 2   9. 22   11. 34   13. 107
2. 0   4. 73   6. 3   8. 2   10. 0   12. 96   14. 45

SATURDAY Page 126   Predators Gone Wild

Forest	Mice	Owls	Ratio	Prediction
A. 4 x 10¹ mice, 2 x 10¹ owls	40	20	2:1	Go hungry
B. 9 x 10¹ mice, 2 x 10¹ owls	90	20	9:2	Go hungry
C. 16 x 10² mice, 1 x 10² owls	1600	100	16:1	Survive
D. 12 x 10⁴ mice, 12 x 10³ owls	120,000	12,000	10:1	Survive
E. 14 x 10² mice, 7 x 10¹ owls	1,400	70	20:1	Survive
F. 21 x 10² mice, 3 x 10² owls	2,100	300	7:1	Go hungry
G. 6 x 10² mice, 4 x 10¹ owls	600	40	15:1	Survive
H. 3 x 10³ mice, 3 x 10¹ owls	3,000	30	100:1	Survive
I. 7 x 10⁴ mice, 8 x 10³ owls	70,000	8,000	8.75:1	Go hungry
J. 8 x 10⁴ mice, 4 x 10² owls	80,000	400	200:1	Survive
K. 5 x 10³ mice, 5 x 10² owls	5,000	500	10:1	Survive
L. 3 x 10³ mice, 7 x 10² owls	3,000	700	4.285:1	Go hungry

SATURDAY Page 127
Hunting with the Lynx!

Year	# of Lynx (in thousands)	# of Hare
1950	79	19,750
1955	41	10,250
1960	160	40,000
1965	37	9,250
1970	100	25,000
1975	12	3,000
1980	140	35,000
1985	21	5,250
1990	90	22,500
1995	14	3,500

Average number of lynx   1950–1995 69.4

Average number of hare   1950–1995 17,350

Range of lynx   1950–1995 12–160

Range of hare   1950–1995 3,000–40,000

SUNDAY Page 128
More Mega Math

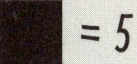 = 5    = 4   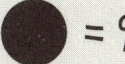 = 9

Answer: ? = 18

Number Puzzle Box

8	10	3	13	34
1	15	6	12	34
9	7	14	4	34
16	2	11	5	34
34	34	34	34	

SUNDAY Page 129
Math Quiz

1. c   2. b   3. a   4. c

WEEK 10 • Pages 130–143

MONDAY Page 131
Activity 10

Answers will vary. Possible responses:
1. She turned it on and aimed it through the window.
2. He lifted the rear window of the truck.
3. He waved the light in the bears' faces, shouted at them, and then pounded on the tailgate of the truck.
4. One bear hit the side of the truck and scratched the side of the bed.
5. The truck was dented and the bed rail was scratched.
6. The cooler was destroyed and the water jug was punctured.

Manobozho Story
You Found The Ending

Manobozho wanted to rebuild the land, but he couldn't because he didn't have any soil. So the beaver dove deep into the water to find soil, but she never returned. Then the otter tried, but he, too, never returned. Everyone on the raft began to despair.

Then the muskrat dove deep into the water and was gone a long time. But then she appeared at the raft, struggling, and opened her paws. There! A tiny little speck of soil!

Manobozho dried the tiny bit of soil in the sun and then blew it into the water. It grew and grew into a great land so that all the waters disappeared.

Ever since that time, Indians have held the beaver, the otter, and the muskrat in the highest honor.

TUESDAY Page 133
Matching

1. d   3. e   5. f   7. a
2. h   4. g   6. b   8. c

WEDNESDAY Page 134
All Boxed In!

1. 144   4. 312   7. 1,150
2. 132   5. 314   8. 472
3. 440   6. 286   9. 1,012

WEDNESDAY Page 135
Mega Math

The wool sweater costs $52.00.
Vowels are worth $8.00 each and consonants are worth $2.00 each.

Riddles

1. A blink   2. A beetle

THURSDAY Page 136
Word Pictures

A. walking side by side
B. oysters on the half shell
C. in between a rock and a hard place
D. eating on the run
E. once upon a time
F. down under
G. broken heart
H. downtown

FRIDAY Page 139
Very Able with Variables

1. Y = $1.60   5. Y = $8.20   9. X = 8   13. X = 20
2. Y = $2.20   6. Y = $11.80   10. X = 9   14. X = 22
3. Y = $4.00   7. Y = $13.00   11. X = 15
4. Y = $7.00   8. X = 3   12. X = 17

SATURDAY Page 140
Planting New Seeds

1. c   3. e   5. d   7. h   9. g
2. f   4. b   6. a   8. j   10. i

WEEK 10 • Continued

SATURDAY Page 141
Too Many Geese!

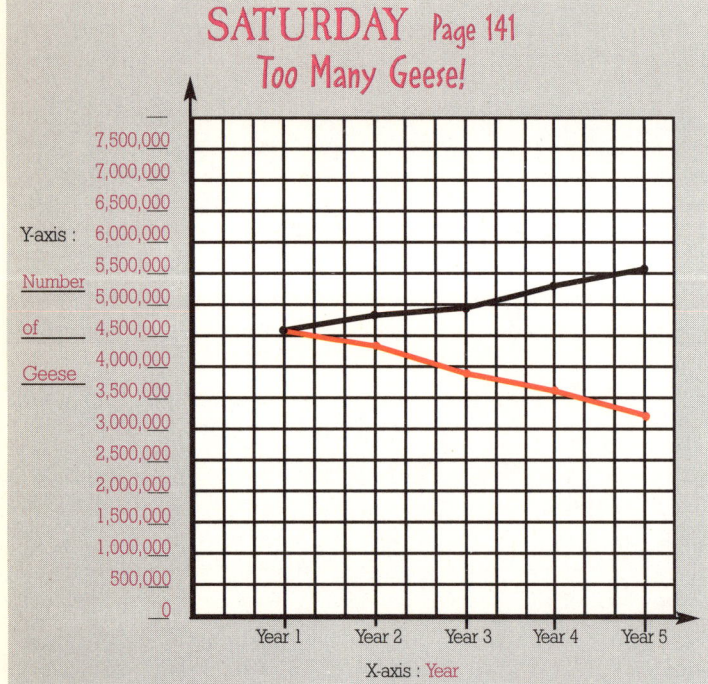

Y-axis : Number of Geese

X-axis : Year

Year 1	4,500,000 geese	Year 1	4,500,000 geese
Year 2	4,725,000 geese	Year 2	4,140,000 geese
Year 3	4,961,250 geese	Year 3	3,808,800 geese
Year 4	5,209,313 geese	Year 4	3,504,096 geese
Year 5	5,469,778 geese	Year 5	3,223,768 geese

SUNDAY Page 142
Odd Number Out

1. $\frac{6}{27}$ 2. $\frac{24}{100}$ 3. $\frac{30}{211}$

Cause and Effect Page 142

1. Cause: **Sam failed his science test.**
   Effect: **Sam couldn't watch television for a week.**

2. Cause: Ellen's grandma was very sick.
   Effect: Ellen made a get-well card.

3. Cause: Rick's hair was hanging in his eyes.
   Effect: Rick got a haircut.

4. Cause: Amber loved to draw.
   Effect: Amber's mom got her art lessons.

WEEK 11 • Pages 144–157

MONDAY Page 145
Activity 11

1. g   3. e   5. d   7. b
2. f   4. c   6. h   8. a

TUESDAY Page 146
Math Maze

Answer: $84 \div 14 = 6 \times 30 = 180$
$32 \times 45 = 1440 \div 8 = 180$

Antonyms, Synonyms or Homonyms

1. synonym   3. homonym   5. synonym
2. antonym   4. homonym   6. antonym

TUESDAY Page 147
Matching

1. e   3. f   5. c   7. d
2. g   4. h   6. a   8. b

WEDNESDAY Page 148
Frightening Freight

1. 336   3. 350   5. 357   7. 196
2. 630   4. 182   6. 385

WEDNESDAY Page 149
Mega Math

Kana has these bills:

6 twenties	$ 120.00
12 tens	$ 120.00
3 fives	$ 15.00
2 ones	$ 2.00
TOTAL	$ 257.00

Line Graph

THURSDAY Page 150
Show Us The Money!

1. $7.43
2. $360.80
3. $11.86
4. $33.11
5. $26.40
6. $17.26

THURSDAY Page 151
Crazy Connections!

1. but (E)
2. but (C)
3. for (A)
4. but (F)
5. yet (B)
6. and (D)

FRIDAY Page 153
Un-Bear-able!

1. R=34   2. H=6   3. G=8   4. U=2   5. Y=12   6. N=43

H U N G R Y

SATURDAY Page 154
Positives and Negatives!

1. Positive, 7
2. Positive, 1
3. Neutral, 0
4. Neutral, 0
5. Negative, −22
6. Negative, −8
7. Positive, 39
8. Negative, −1
9. Negative, −13
10. Positive, 75

Total for the page:
Positive, 78

SATURDAY Page 155
Pay Dirt!

1. −1,063   Granite
2. 229   Clay
3. −1,310   Lodestone
4. 98   Quartz
5. −1,945   Sludge
6. −463   Shale
7. 173   Clay
8. −308   Limestone
9. −2,069   Sludge
10. −1,399   Lodestone

SUNDAY Page 156
More Mega Math

$\blacksquare = 3$ $\blacktriangle = 7$ $\bullet = 2$

Answer: ? = 14

Missing Math

$3^{(2)} = 9$ $2 \times 4 = 8$

$6 + 1 = 7$ $5 = \dfrac{25}{5}$

SUNDAY Page 157
Word Problems

1. $700,000 \times .8 = 560,000$ T-shirts
2. $528 \div 24 = 22$ students
3. 8hr − 1hr = 7hrs × 2 = 14 rides
4. 52 weeks in a year
   × 2
   104 gallons of milk
5. 76.00   169.00
   +40.00   → −116.00
   $116.00 $53.00
6. 10:6   14 wins,   6 losses   BEST
         10 wins,   10 losses   WORST

Page 159
Activity 12

4, 10, 1, 6, 7, 2, 8, 5, 3, 9

How to solve
Grid Logic problems...

Grid logic is a fun way to figure out what traits or facts should be paired together, based on a series of clues that have been given. The key part of solving a grid logic problem is the grid. As you read the questions, use the grid to mark with an "X" traits that you know don't go together. For example, if the clue is "Emily and the Phillips child live near each other," you can put an X in the box that pairs "Emily" and "Phillips" together, because you now know they are two separate people. Make sure to pay close attention to the clues that are given. For example, if the clue says, "the Turner boy..." you know to mark an "X" by any girl's name that intersects with Turner. The clue just told you that the Turner child is a boy, not a girl. If you know that two traits DO go together, you can mark the intersecting box with an "O." The following is an example of a grid logic problem. Let's solve it together.

Mary and her friends went to the pool. While they were there, they each swam laps using a different stroke. Based on the clues below, can you determine each child's first and last name and the type of stroke they used?

1. Mary and the Waters girl both ride their bikes to the pool.
2. The boy who swam the breaststroke has the same initial for his first and last name.
3. The child who swam freestyle, Mary, and the Holland child all live in the same neighborhood.
4. Christopher swam a stroke named after an insect.

	Mary	Cecily	Christopher	Jon	Backstroke	Freestyle	Breaststroke	Butterfly
Jones								
Waters								
Holland								
Warner								
Backstroke								
Freestyle								
Breaststroke								
Butterfly								

1. **Mary and the Waters girl both ride their bikes to the pool.**

   This clue tells us that Mary's last name is not Waters, so we place an "X" in the box that intersects "Mary" and "Waters." It also tells us that the Waters child is a girl, so we can also place an "X" in the boxes that intersect "Waters" with "Christopher" and "Jon," because they are not girls.

   By doing that, it is clear that the Waters child is Cecily, so we can place an "O" in that box. We can also place an "X" in the boxes that cross Cecily with the other last names: Jones, Holland, and Warner.

2. **The boy who swam the breaststroke has the same initial for his first and last name.**

   The only first and last names that have the same initial are "Jon" and "Jones," so we can place an "O" in that box and an "X" in the others.

   We can also place an "O" in the boxes that intersect "Jon" and "Jones" with "breaststroke."

3. **The child who swam freestyle, Mary, and the Holland child all live in the same neighborhood.**

   This clue tells us that Mary's last name is not Holland. By placing an "X" in that box, we find out that Mary's last name is Warner and Christopher's is Holland.

   It also tells us that Mary (Warner) and (Christopher) Holland did not swim freestyle. By crossing out those boxes, we discover that it was Cecily who swam freestyle.

4. **Christopher swam a stroke named after an insect.**

   The only stroke named after an insect is the "butterfly" and this clue tells us that Christopher is the one who swam it. After matching "Christopher" with the "butterfly," we discover that Mary is the child who swam the backstroke.

   The grid is now complete and it gives us these answers: Mary Warner swam backstroke, Cecily Waters swam freestyle, Christopher Holland swam butterfly, and Jon Jones swam breaststroke.

	Mary	Cecily	Christopher	Jon	Backstroke	Freestyle	Breaststroke	Butterfly
Jones								
Waters	X		X	X				
Holland								
Warner								
Backstroke								
Freestyle								
Breaststroke								
Butterfly								

	Mary	Cecily	Christopher	Jon	Backstroke	Freestyle	Breaststroke	Butterfly
Jones		X						
Waters	X	O	X	X				
Holland		X						
Warner		X						
Backstroke								
Freestyle								
Breaststroke								
Butterfly								

	Mary	Cecily	Christopher	Jon	Backstroke	Freestyle	Breaststroke	Butterfly
Jones	X	X	X	O				
Waters	X	O	X	X				
Holland		X		X				
Warner		X		X				
Backstroke								
Freestyle								
Breaststroke								
Butterfly								

	Mary	Cecily	Christopher	Jon	Backstroke	Freestyle	Breaststroke	Butterfly
Jones	X	X	X	O	X	X	O	X
Waters	X	O	X	X			X	
Holland		X		X			X	
Warner		X		X			X	
Backstroke				X				
Freestyle				X				
Breaststroke	X	X	X	O				
Butterfly				X				

	Mary	Cecily	Christopher	Jon	Backstroke	Freestyle	Breaststroke	Butterfly
Jones	X	X	X	O	X	X	O	X
Waters	X	O	X	X	X	O	X	X
Holland	X	X	O	X		X	X	
Warner	O	X	X	X	X	X		
Backstroke		X		X				
Freestyle	X	O	X	X				
Breaststroke	X	X	X	O				
Butterfly		X		X				

	Mary	Cecily	Christopher	Jon	Backstroke	Freestyle	Breaststroke	Butterfly
Jones	X	X	X	O	X	X	O	X
Waters	X	O	X	X	X	O	X	X
Holland	X	X	O	X	X	X	X	O
Warner	O	X	X	X	O	X	X	X
Backstroke	O	X	X	X				
Freestyle	X	O	X	X				
Breaststroke	X	X	X	O				
Butterfly	X	X	O	X				

Answer:
Mary Warner/Backstroke
Cecily Waters/Freestyle
Christopher Holland/Butterfly
Jon Jones/Breaststroke

Greatest Common Factor

A factor is a number that divides evenly (with no remainder) into another. The largest factor shared by two or more numbers is the Greatest Common Factor (GCF).

For example:

16 can be divided evenly by 16, 8, 4, 2 and 1
24 can be divided evenly by 24, 12, 8, 6, 4, 2 and 1

The GCF is 8 because it is the largest shared factor.

Using a Protractor

A protractor is a tool for measuring the size (in degrees) of an angle. To use it correctly, you must put the protractor directly along one line of an angle and make sure the exact center of the bottom of the protractor (usually marked with a "0") is placed exactly at the base of the angle.

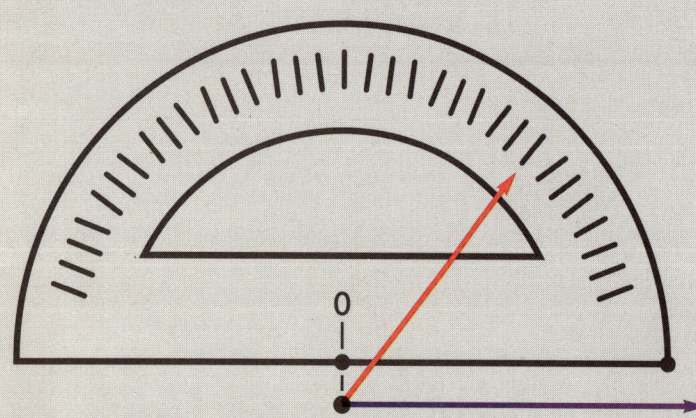

While one line of the angle now runs along the bottom of the protractor, the other points toward a number on the arc of the protractor. (You may need to use a ruler to help you determine the exact number it is pointing toward.)

Notice that the numbers (1 – 180) go in both directions. This lets you measure angles that open on either side.

Super Duper Chopper Copter

Top

Bottom

EXPLORING FLIGHT

EXPLORING FLIGHT

ORVILLE & WILBUR WRIGHT
(1871–1948, 1867–1912)

Wilbur and Orville Wright were two brothers who shared a sense of ingenuity and a common dream. During the late 19th century, the idea of flight seemed ridiculous and was actually very dangerous. Many early flight aviators died in their attempts, but the Wright brothers were convinced they could do it. They were so convinced that they gave up any idea of a social life, or marriage, so that they could concentrate all their energies on the flight quest.

The two brothers began with experiments on gliders, but what they really longed to achieve was controlled flight by a machine that used its own power, not the power of the wind. After many experiments, the Wright brothers were ready for their first engine-powered flight. They chose to test their "flying machine" in December, 1903, in Kitty Hawk, North Carolina. The first flight ended in mishap when a part called the skid snapped. Three days later, airplane fixed, Orville made the historic flight. It only lasted 12 seconds, but it was the first time in history that a self-powered machine carried a man forward into free flight, without losing speed, and landed without injury. Those 12 seconds marked the beginning of modern aviation.

AMELIA EARHART
(1897–1937)

No one will ever know exactly what happened to Amelia Earhart. Earhart was the first person to fly from Hawaii to California. She was the first woman to fly cross-country over the United States. As a young girl, Earhart had always wanted to go higher and faster. She'd even built a modified roller coaster in her backyard.

She wanted to be the first to fly around the widest part of the world—the equator. She set off with her navigator, Fred Noonan, and the two began their journey, first from Miami to San Juan, Puerto Rico. Stopping at different sites along the way, they flew over Africa, India, Australia, and made it to New Guinea. The next leg of their journey was to get to Howland, a tiny island surrounded by miles of ocean. She never made it. Radio contact was lost and search crews were unable to find any sign of her or her plane.

CHARLES LINDBERGH
(1902–1974)

Charles Lindbergh flew his plane, the "Spirit of St. Louis," from New York to Paris in 33 hours. It was the first solo transatlantic flight.

As a young man, Lindbergh was a "barnstormer." Barnstormers were daredevils who charged set prices for stunts like head-on collisions with cars, crashing planes into trees, and flying upside down with a man on the landing gear.

As an airmail pilot, between Chicago and St. Louis, Lindbergh heard about a $25,000 prize for the first person to complete a flight across the Atlantic Ocean without stopping. Some St. Louis businessmen invested in the project and the Ryan Aircraft company built the "Spirit of St. Louis."

Taking off from New York, Lindbergh carried only a compass, four sandwiches, two canteens of water, 451 gallons (1707 liters) of gas and a chart balanced on his knees. During the flight, he battled fatigue and bone-chilling cold. There was no heater and Lindbergh flew low over icebergs and the vast Atlantic Ocean. He landed in Paris, on May 21, 1927, as a celebrity. He was only 25 years old. After the historic flight, his life was marked by controversy and tragedy.

THE HINDENBURG
"Oh, the Humanity"

The Hindenburg was a famous dirigible. A dirigible (or zeppelin) was a flying machine made of several balloons inside a rigid structure. These balloons were filled with hydrogen, an extremely flammable fuel. Zeppelins were huge structures. At a length of 803 feet (244.8 m), the Hindenburg was almost the length of the Titanic. It remains the largest airship to ever have cruised the skies.

Tickets for the flight were $400, the price of a small car in those days. For that price, passengers were fed freshly prepared food, slept in their own rooms and could even shower.

The Hindenburg left Germany, carrying 61 crew members and 36 passengers. It flew over the airfield in New Jersey for a routine landing. Suddenly, something ignited the hydrogen that filled the great balloons. It took only seconds for the burning Hindenburg to crash to the ground. Twenty-two crewmen, 13 passengers, and one member of the ground crew died. Radio reporter, Herb Morrison, watching from the ground, cried, "It's burst into flames...Get out of the way please!...Oh, the humanity, and all the passengers..."

EXPLORING

FLIGHT

EXPLORING FLIGHT

JACKIE COCHRAN
(Around 1906-1980)

She didn't own a pair of shoes until she was eight, but by the time Jackie Cochran died, she'd held more aviation records than anyone, male or female, in speed, altitude and distance. As a child, she often slept on the floor and went hungry. Cochran was giving permanent waves in a beauty salon by the time she was thirteen. Years later, while living in New York City, a friend suggested she learn to fly. As soon as she took her first lesson, Jackie Cochran knew she was an aviator. She began entering contests and winning them. She was the first woman to pilot a military bomber across the Atlantic Ocean. She founded the WASPs (Women's Airforce Service Pilots) during WWII, and was awarded the Distinguished Service Medal for her actions during WWII. After the war, she was the first woman to break the sound barrier. Other pilots looked at Jackie Cochran as a pilot who wasn't there for the glory—she was just trying to see how fast she could go.

CHUCK YEAGER
(1923–present)

In 1947, the agency that would become NASA tested a plane they thought could go faster than the speed of sound (around 650 mph or 1046 kmph). Chuck Yeager, a test pilot, was experienced and cool under pressure. At 20,000 feet (6096 m) the X-1 was released from the B-29 that carried it (built for speed, the X-1 was only able to fly for 3 minutes, so it needed another craft to get it to a higher altitude). The machmeter, used to measure the plane's speed, seemed to go haywire. It was made to go up to Mach 1. Yeager went up to Mach 1.07. He was the first to go faster than the speed of sound.

THE CONCORDE

The Concorde was a supersonic plane that traveled at speeds of about 1,490 miles (2,398 km) per hour—more than twice the speed of sound! A Boeing 747 has a top speed of 604 miles (972 km) per hour. At its cruising altitude of 60,000 feet (18,288 m), passengers could see the curvature of the earth! A regular jet takes about 8 hours to get from New York to London. The Concord made the same trip in less than 3 hours. Commercial service began in 1976 and ended in 2003 due to the high cost of maintaining the planes.

THE STEALTH BOMBER

Radar technology makes it possible to locate the position, shape and often speed of an airplane. Objects reflect radio waves the same way they reflect light. The way a particular object reflects radio waves is called a radar signature. Although its wingspan is half the size of a football field, the B-2 Stealth Bomber is virtually invisible to radar because of its reduced radar signature. Many other features that make the B-2 Stealth Bomber "stealthy" are classified by the U.S. Government.

JOHN GLENN JR.
(1921–present)

John Glenn was a member of the original group of NASA astronauts, the Mercury Seven. (M. Scott Carpenter, L. Gordon Cooper, Jr., Virgil (Gus) Grissom, Walter M. (Wally) Schirra Jr., Alan B. Shepard, Jr., and Donald K. (Deke) Slayton.) On February 20, 1962, Glenn became the first American to orbit the Earth. After 4 hours, 55 minutes and 23 seconds, and 3 rotations around the Earth, Glenn landed the Friendship 7 safely in the Pacific Ocean. After his time as an astronaut, Glenn was successful in politics. In 1998, the 77-year-old Glenn went up in space again, as a member of the space shuttle Discovery.

THE MOON LANDING

On July 20, 1969, people all over the world gathered in front of their televisions, near their radios, and in each other's homes. Mankind was crossing the final frontier. The Apollo 11 entered the moon's orbit. Neil Armstrong and Edwin "Buzz" Aldrin boarded the Eagle, a landing craft designed to take them to the moon's surface. Michael Collins stayed behind, in the command module. Six and a half hours later, Armstrong was the first to crawl out of the capsule. As his boots touched the moon's surface, he said, "That's one small step for man—one giant leap for mankind."

INTERNATIONAL SPACE STATION

The International Space Station is being built by 16 different countries: the United States, Canada, Russia, Brazil, Japan and a group of nations known as the European Space Agency (Belgium, Britain, Denmark, France, Germany, Italy, Norway, Spain, Sweden, Switzerland and the Netherlands). Life on the ISS is very different from life on Earth. Astronauts witness 15 dawns per day. They have to attach their sleeping bags to a wall to keep from floating into station equipment. Dinner is sometimes soup served in plastic bags. At the end of a busy day, astronauts can look out on the view that makes it all worth it: the Earth rotating on its axis.